Our Own Rascals First

Our Own Rascals First

Inclusion and Exclusion in the Use of Sanctions

Inaugural lecture
as Chair in Penology & Penitentiary Law at
Rijksuniversiteit Groningen,
delivered on 21 February 2012

by

prof. dr. M.M. Boone

eleven
international publishing

Published, sold and distributed by Eleven International Publishing
P.O. Box 85576
2508 CG The Hague
The Netherlands
Tel.: +31 70 33 070 33
Fax: +31 70 33 070 30
e-mail: sales@budh.nl
www.elevenpub.com

Sold and distributed in USA and Canada
International Specialized Book Services
920 NE 58th Avenue, Suite 300
Portland, OR 97213-3786, USA
Tel: 1-800-944-6190 (toll-free)
Fax: +1 503 280-8832
orders@isbs.com
www.isbs.com

Eleven International Publishing is an imprint of Boom uitgevers Den Haag.

ISBN 978-94-90947-96-5

Cover image: Constant, Labyrismen 11, 1968.

Printed in The Netherlands

Table of Contents

The Honourable Vice-Chancellor, Ladies and Gentlemen,

In 2011, A bill was presented to the Lower House of the Dutch Parliament, introducing minimum sentences for repeat offenders of the most heinous crimes. In response to the bill, which is still only an initial draft, the Council for the Administration of Criminal Law and the Protection of Youth (*Raad voor Strafrechtstoepassing en Jeugdbescherming, RSJ*) noted that no reference to the idea of resocializing prison inmates could be found in the bill. As regards the toughest group of repeat offenders, first and foremost, the proposal meant longer penalization. The Council called this surprising, especially since penal policy is in other aspects so much focused on the possibility of resocialization (RSJ 2011, p. 2).

The Council pointed out a typical example of what Cavadino and Dignan, in their influential comparative penology study on penal systems all across the globe, call *bifurcation*, the strategy of developing and enforcing lighter sentences for less serious offenders, and new and more severe sentences for offenders viewed as especially bad or dangerous (Cavadino and Dignan 2006, *e.g.*, see p. 68). They cite the Netherlands as a country where the penetration of bifurcation has been especially extensive. Although political developments in the Netherlands might lead one to expect it to have shifted as a whole from a humane and inclusive penal strategy to a tougher and more exclusive one, in their view this has not been the case. And I quote, 'What has happened has been more like a redrawing of the boundaries of the community – to exclude offenders viewed as incorrigible lost souls, but still include less serious (…) offenders' (Cavadino & Dignan 2006, pp. 120-121). In this inaugural lecture, I will focus on this issue of inclusion and exclusion, particularly as regards the situation in the Netherlands. I shall demonstrate that though there is indeed evidence of a division in the use of sanctions, it has not solely or even mainly been along the border between severe and less severe or dangerous offenders. I will make an effort to explain how bifurcation has manifested itself in the Dutch penal framework at a macro-sociological level as well as from a micro-perspective and formulate a normative evaluation based on the legal principles for sentencing. My story is solely based on the sentencing of adult offenders.

Hard and Soft Sentences

Instead of *hard* and *soft* sentences, Cavadino and Dignan refer to *inclusive* and *exclusive* ones. The aim of inclusive sentences is to keep offenders in society or provide a position for them there via re-integrative activities. Exclusive are sentences that keep offenders from taking part in society and that are not focused on preparing them to return there. This division is not renowned for its clarity, but my line of reasoning does not require a very precise system of classification. It is clear that in recent decades, the Netherlands has become more differentiated in both directions, starting with the more severe side.

Although the total number of prison inmates in the Netherlands has decreased in the past few years, in the same period there has been a substantial increase in the average length of the prison sentences enforced for what are viewed as the most severe crimes.[1] Van Tulder calculates that since 2000, violent crimes have been penalized 20% more severely (Van Tulder 2011, p. 1545).[2] The average sentence for rape and other sexual crimes increased between 2000 and 2009 by almost 40% (Van Tulder 2011, p. 1545). The increase in the number of life sentences should also be noted. Between 1970 and 1990, three offenders were sentenced to life in prison without parole, but the same held true of no fewer than twenty-nine offenders between 1990 and July 2011, twenty-two of whom in the past ten years (Forum Levenslang, July 2011). What is more, the life sentence has become considerably more severe since the policy of pardoning *lifers* if possible was abandoned (Forum Levenslang, June 2010, p. 3).

For offenders not legally accountable for their acts, a provision has also been created to make it possible to incarcerate them for longer periods of time. In 1999, the first long-stay ward was opened for offenders sentenced to detention under a hospital order and categorized as untreatable. In the past, offenders sentenced to detention under a hospital order could only be transferred to a long-stay ward after having been treated intramurally for at least six years (RSJ 2008b, p. 57). Nowadays, they can be recommended for selection at a long-stay ward if according to present standards, they have 'undergone all the treatment options' (RSJ 2008, p. 61). The number of offenders sentenced to detention under a hospital order who are now at a long-stay ward is fourteen times of what it was when the wards opened in 1999 (RSJ 2008b, p. 15); the figure rose from 21 in 1999 to 200 in 2010 (Dienst Justitiële Inrichtingen, DJI, p. 19).

It is also typical of bifurcation that there are separate regimes for categories of offenders viewed as the most criminal or dangerous. Cavadino and Dignan call the maximum security prison in Vught a typical example of the Dutch bifurcation strategy. This prison is designed for convicts who – either because they have actually demonstrated the intention to escape or because their escape would cause a great deal of

1 Kalidien & De Heer-de Lange (2011), Table 6.16, for example the average prison sentence for fatal crimes rose from 695 to 890 days.
2 The average length of non-suspended prison sentences for homicide and manslaughter increased between 1993 and 2004 from 6.3 to 8.9 years (Van Wingerden & Nieuwbeerta 2006, p. 33).

social unrest – are classified as a flight risk.[3] To prevent them from escaping, a regime has been created that is referred to as 'unprecedentedly strict' (Cavadino & Dignan 2006, p. 126), not only in the Dutch context but also in an international framework. No activities are allowed in groups of more than two inmates, they can only see their visitors from behind glass and they are regularly handcuffed and searched all over, including anally, to check for illegal substances.

This category is also incarcerated at the terrorist ward for inmates suspected and convicted of terrorist crimes. The terrorist ward was opened in 2005 to keep this category of inmates from spreading their radical ideas among the rest of the prison population. They are not only isolated from prisoners not serving sentences for terrorist acts, but also subjected to an extremely limited regime and usually have to take part alone in what few activities are organized for them. There are no facilities for detention phasing or resocialization. After an extremely critical evaluation, at the moment, the terrorist ward is not actually being used (Boone 2009, Sackers 2011, Veldhuis *et al.* 2010).

It is possible to defend the lengthy sentences and severe regimes I have just described by saying they are designed for offenders who have committed the most heinous crimes, but this certainly does not hold true for some other regimes characterized by austerity and the absence of any activities focused on returning to society. It does not hold true, for example, for the detention centres opened in such a rush in 2002 to cope with the mass arrival of drug couriers at Amsterdam Airport Schiphol. While cell-sharing was an exception in the Netherlands until that time, it was introduced on a large scale for this particular category of offenders. In any number of ways, the regime departed from the regular one, there were no facilities for engaging in sports, attending courses or even going to a library, let alone reintegrating into society (Boone 2006). The detention centres have since become mainly populated by foreigners about to be deported and offenders who are to leave the country after serving their sentences.

In 2008, a separate regime was developed for this last category of prison inmates with no residence permit to stay in the Netherlands after their release.[4] The argument in favour of separate incarceration of this group is that the focus is not on resocialization after their release nor on related issues such as short leaves, regionalization or

3 Art. 6 Regeling selectie, plaatsing en overplaatsing van gedetineerden (Section 6 Regulation on the Selection, Placement and Transfer of Prison Inmates) 15 augustus 2000, nr. 5042803/00/DJI, Stcrt. 2000, 176, recently adapted by regulation 27-7-2011, nr. 5672146/10/DJI, Stcrt. 2011, 14766.

4 Section 20b, Regeling selectie, plaatsing en overplaatsing gedetineerden.

detention phasing.[5] For this group as well, prison conditions are considerably more austere than for other inmates. There can barely be any differentiation among them and the quality of psychological care is poorer than for regular prisoners. Here again, barely any activities are organized and no activities at all focused on returning to society. The systematic detention in shared cells sometimes leads to unsafe situations (RSJ 2010).[6]

In the direction of the soft side, there has also been considerable differentiation and liberalization. In the early 1980s, enthusiastic steps were taken to develop alternatives for imprisonment now known as community service. The aim was to reduce the harmful effects of imprisonment and enlarge the resocialization potential of the sentencing framework. In a later stage, other objectives were added, like for example the reinforcement of the credibility of the criminal justice system (Boone 2010). In 2010, almost 30,000 adults alone were sentenced to community service (Kalidien & De Heer-de Lange 2011, p. 178).

The title of the inaugural lecture by Professor Tulkens, one of my predecessors at this university, was *Degrees of Freedom*, an expression that was referring to prison inmates' gradual return to society (Tulkens 2011). When the Penitentiary Principles Act was passed in 1999, penitentiary programmes were introduced in this framework enabling inmates to spend the last phase of their detention outside prison with or without an electronic ankle cuff and take part in rehabilitative activities under the supervision of the Dutch Probation Office.[7]

In 2002, the Push Back Recidivism Programme was introduced in the Probation Service and the Prison Service. The introduction of this programme meant a radical change regarding the notion of resocialization. Ever since, all clients of the Probation Service and inmates with more than four months of a non-suspended prison sentence remaining are subjected to a structured diagnosis of their recidivism risk, the causes of their criminality, and their learning styles. The outcome can lead to behavioural interventions designed to considerably reduce the risk of recidivism and facilitate a return

5 This assumption is permanently erroneous, as has often been noted (Boone 2003, Van Kalmthout 2007). The Dutch Supreme Court had already decreed in 1987 that the resocialization aim should not be solely restricted to inmates who are to return to society after their release (Supreme Court, 16 January 1987, Netherlands Jurisprudence 1987, no. 405).

6 Also Premininy against Russia, European Court for Human Rights, 10 February 2011, European Human Rights Cases 10 June 2011, no. 6, pp. 919-936, with note by M. Boone.

7 If the ideas of the outgoing State Secretary of Security and Justice about detention phasing are put into effect, the penitentiary programme will soon be terminated, Parliamentary Documents II, 2010-2011, 29 270, no. 52, p. 5.

to society. This can be done either in the final detention phase or in the framework of a suspended sentence or measure.

For the past few years, ardent efforts have once again been made to replace short non-suspended prison sentences with suspended sentences under special conditions providing better opportunities to influence behaviour.[8] To stimulate judges to make more frequent use of the special conditions, a bill was recently passed more firmly embedding them in the law.[9] Also, the supervision of the Probation Service on the compliance of special conditions by a conditional sanction has been radically changed (Poort 2009).

Bifurcation

How does bifurcation work? Along what lines? Who undergoes the inclusive sanctions and who do the exclusive ones pertain to? To answer these questions, I have collected data on the application criteria of most of the sanctions and features of the individuals they apply to. I have devoted special attention to the crimes committed, the criminal history, the countries where offenders were born and the requirements regarding their motivation and mastery of the Dutch language. I would like to present the most striking results.

It is clear by now that the most austere regimes are reserved for offenders not born in the Netherlands or not residents, the drug couriers and foreigners with no legal right to live in the Netherlands after they serve their sentences. Almost half the inmates serving their sentence under an ordinary prison regime were also born outside the Netherlands, something only true of 12% of the entire Dutch population (Department of Forensic Institutions 2010, p. 23, Verhagen 2011, p. 22). The country of birth only partially explains 'the overwhelming black colour of the Dutch prison population', as Downes and Van Swaaningen (2007) put it, since it does not make clear what percentage of the prison population has one or two parents born abroad.[10] The over-representation of ethnic minority prison inmates is partly what inspired the title of this inaugural lecture, but only partly, since the prison population also appears to substantially deviate from the average Dutch population in a number of other ways. Jos Verhagen has recently listed a number of features of prison inmates based on the Recidivism Assessment Scales (RISc) the Dutch Probation Office and

8 Parliamentary Documents II, 2009-2010, 32 319, no. 3, p. 1.

9 Statute Book 2011, no. 615.

10 Of course the approximately 1,200 foreigners awaiting deportation at Dutch penal facilities are not included in this percentage. In this inaugural lecture, I am talking about rascals, and foreigners awaiting deportation are definitely not in this category, even though the incarceration denying them their freedom might give a different impression (DJI 2011c).

Prison Department use for screening offenders (Verhagen 2011).[11] Approximately half the prisoners are characterized as problematic drug users (Verhagen 2011, p. 96). Only a quarter of the prisoners were gainfully employed shortly before their detention and a third never worked at any time in their lives. Half the prisoners have more debts than they would be able to pay back with the income they have. In the past, the Health Council and other agencies have observed that approximately 6% of the prison population suffer from psychotic disorders, 14%-35% have depressions and approximately half of them exhibit some antisocial personality disorder. These percentages are all much higher than the normal prevalence in society (Council for the Administration of Criminal Law and the Protection of Youth 2007). It has more recently been acknowledged that many offenders are mentally handicapped, and the percentage of mentally handicapped prison inmates is estimated at 20%-25% (RSJ 2008a).

Who populates the maximum security prison? There is not a great deal of information available about the background of the inmates incarcerated at the maximum security prison since 1994. It can however be deduced from the selection criteria that the regime at the maximum security prison is not necessarily intended for suspects and convicts who commit the most heinous crimes, so the situation does not coincide with the rather slipshod division into the two groups specified by Cavadino and Dignan. After all, the prison inmates planning to escape are not necessarily the ones who committed the most serious crimes, and this certainly does not hold true of prisoners only incarcerated at the maximum security prison in Vught because their escape would lead to so much social unrest. In our shadow evaluation of the Penitentiary Principles Act passed in 2001, De Jonge and I noted that an extradition request can play an important role in the decision whether or not to hold or incarcerate an individual at the maximum security prison (Boone & De Jonge 2001, p. 18).

As a result of the extremely well-thought-out evaluation by behavioural science researchers at the University of Groningen, we know more about the terrorist ward inmates. Inmates suspected or convicted of a terrorist crime or who express or publicize a radical message prior to or during their detention can be placed at a terrorist ward.[12] In actual practice, inmates are only incarcerated at a terrorist ward on the basis of the first two criteria (Veldhuis *et al.* 2010, p. 121). From the opening of the terror-

11 There can be serious doubts as to whether this is an adequate instrument for describing the prison population. No matter how much of a pretence of academic objectivity scores on scales might have, in the end they are still only subjective estimations by probation officers that reflect in part the dominant moral views. This is why I confine myself in my summary to scales that can be relatively objectively determined and I do not devote attention to scales that measure items such as thought and behavioural patterns and emotional well-being.

12 Art. 20a Regeling selectie, plaatsing en overplaatsing van gedetineerden.

ist ward at the prison in Vught in 2006 until the end of June 2010,[13] thirty prisoners were incarcerated at one of the two terrorist wards (Veldhuis *et al.* 2010, p. 116). It is striking that as a result of counter-indications, nine of them were soon transferred to a regular prison,[14] and thirteen immediately released after the judge pronounced the verdict. On average, inmates remain at a terrorist ward for nine months, a sentence not indicative of crimes judged by a criminal court to be extremely heinous. Moreover, this figure is distorted by a small number of inmates serving a lengthy sentence at a terrorist ward. Other striking features of terrorist ward prisoners pertain to their nationality and religious beliefs. Nine of the inmates were born in the Netherlands, and the other twenty-one come from other countries such as Morocco, Turkey, Iraq and Sri Lanka (Veldhuis *et al.* 2010, p. 117). The large majority of the terrorist ward inmates were Muslims (Boone 2007, Veldhuis *et al.* 2010, p. 133), although non-Muslims were also incarcerated in the same period for terrorist activities (Veldhuis *et al.* 2010, pp. 120-121). At a later stage, several non-Muslims were incarcerated for a short period at the terrorist ward, but only after critical comments were made about the one-sided composition of the population at the terrorist ward (Veldhuis *et al.* 2010, p. 133).

And to whom are the sentences at the other end of the spectrum, the soft, inclusive ones given to? This is a question often approached from the other side, namely who is excluded from the soft, rehabilitative sentences? A recurrent point of criticism is that they are only given to the most privileged category of offenders. Socially weak offenders are thought to be excluded from these sentences (Kelk 1998, Nelissen 2001), as are unmotivated offenders (Fiselier 1998, Kelk 1998, Reidnied 2001) and ethnic minority offenders (Boone 2002). In short, offenders who are given inclusive sentences are the mirror image of the offenders incarcerated in a closed setting. This impression has recently been confirmed as regards the various sentences I describe as inclusive. I shall discuss three of them.

It is a known fact that offenders with a Dutch background are sentenced to community service much more frequently than offenders with a foreign background. Wermink *et al.* noted that offenders sentenced to community service are five times as likely to have been born in the Netherlands (Wermink *et al.* 2009) as offenders sentenced to a short period in prison. On the basis of their observation of 365 criminal cases that came before a police court judge, the same group of researchers conclude that suspects who look Dutch and speak Dutch have the least chance of being sentenced to prison

13 The date when the data collection for the evaluation study on the terrorist ward was concluded (Veldhuis *et al.* 2010, p. 116).

14 Veldhuis 2010, p. 118. Six were transferred within a month, two after one or two days, one female inmate was transferred from Vught to De Schie and then to a regular prison.

(Wermink *et al.* 2012). After an earlier study, Lünneman and colleagues conclude that although the percentage of drug addicts and unemployed people is higher among individuals sentenced to community service than among the normal Dutch population (Lünneman *et al.* 2005), it is nonetheless quite a bit lower than among the prison population (Boone 2010).

In 2006 and 2008, the Inspection Service for Implementation of Sanctions completed a study on how penitentiary programmes are put into practice. The Inspection Service notes that one third of the 5,000 prison inmates eligible for a penitentiary programme in 2005 actually ended their incarceration period this way. However, they are mainly prisoners with relatively few problems who do not require any special interventions to present only a limited risk of recidivism. Prison inmates who exhibit problematic behaviour during their incarceration, use drugs or need special care are not selected for a penitentiary programme. These *problematic* prisoners would have benefited from specific interventions or treatments, but they are not selected, the necessary programmes are not made adequately available to them or the risks of failure are estimated as being too high according to the Inspection (Inspection Service for Implementation of Sanctions 2006, *Inspectie voor de Sanctietoepassing*, pp. 33-37).[15]

Recently, Tamar Fischer, Miriam Captein and Barbara Zwirs of the Criminology Department at Erasmus University published the results of their study on exclusion factors in the use of behavioural interventions on adult offenders. They arrive at exclusion factors comparable to those the *Inspection Service on the Use of Sanctions* observed earlier. Insufficient motivation, drug-related problems, limited mental capacity and an inadequate mastery of the Dutch language are some of the relative exclusion factors. Offenders not having a valid Dutch residence permit or still having a short part of their sentence to be served are also reasons for not offering them behavioural interventions. Each of these various exclusion factors plays a role in an average of approximately 25% of the candidates for a Reduction of Recidivism Programme. Whether this does indeed exclude them from participation in a behavioural intervention has not yet been demonstrated though. In actual practice, motivation for example turns out to be used much less strictly as an exclusion criterion than the counter-indications

15 In response to the reaction of the Minister of Justice to these findings (Parliamentary Documents II, 2006-2007, 24 587, no. 198), the Inspection Service for Implementation of Sanctions conducted a sequel study on the question of whether the introduction of the Reduction of Recidivism Programme remedies the shortcomings that the Service observed. This appears to only be the case to a very limited extent. It is true that the Inspection Service does observe more support for the notion that prison inmates who need special care should be eligible for a penitentiary programme than for the notion that they should not be eligible because they are too problematic, but at the same time it concludes that there is no increase in the number of prison inmates admitted to a penitentiary programme despite their observed drug use, and that the chance of being admitted to a penitentiary programme remains considerably smaller for prison inmates with short sentences than for those with longer sentences (Inspectie voor de Sanctietoepassing 2008, pp. 12-13).

for behavioural interventions seem to show. The Dutch Probation Office itself nonetheless works from the assumption that at least a quarter of the candidates eligible for a behavioural intervention based on the results of the Recidivism Assessment Scales are disqualified due to one of the exclusion factors.[16] This is particularly worrisome since the very same study shows that criminogenous factors, which stimulate criminal conduct and should be able to be treated by intervention, occur far more frequently in the group excluded from the interventions.

Macro-Perspective

I have now arrived at the explanatory part of this inaugural lecture. What is the theoretical explanation for inclusion and exclusion and why has it developed along the lines I have described? I shall outline a macro-sociological as well as a micro-perspective.

Exclusion

Various theoreticians link harder and more exclusive sentences or measures to a number of comprehensive changes society has been witnessing. Sociologists like Ulrich Beck, Anthony Giddens, Zygmunt Bauman and Barbara Hudson capture the essence of these changes in catchy phrases, sketching a society that has undergone a total metamorphosis since the 1960s: Emancipation, large-scale immigration and enormous technological advances, as well as widespread crime and nuclear and terrorist threats. The common factor in their explanations is that the huge changes in modern society, the constant movement, what Bauman calls the *fluidity* (Bauman 2000) and the intangibility of the risks they generate make people feel insecure and cling to what is familiar. What is unfamiliar or implies a potential risk is rejected. This is why the authors I mention speak of a *risk society* (Beck 1992, Hudson 2003), an *exclusive society* (Young 1999), a *culture of control* (Garland 2001) or a *scapegoat society* (Beck 1992, Young 1999). On the one hand, the national authorities take advantage of the people's fears, enabling them to win votes by pretending to have solutions to the complex problems confronting the public at large. But they are also overcharged by the people, who see risks approaching that they are no longer able to protect or insure themselves against (Giddens 1990, Beck 1992, Pratt 2005, p. 35). In a divided and fragmented late modern society, nowadays, criminal law – designed as the ultimate remedy, if all else fails to teach individual stubborn recidivists the norms approved by general consensus – is often called upon to stipulate a dominant norm that is not nearly always that clear and to enforce it among those who are (visibly) not agreeable towards it. In the terminology of Boutellier (2002), from *ultimate* to *urgent* criminal law.

16 Penal and Probation System, Analysis of Penitentiary Programmes, 20 October 2011, Draft 2.1.

I went back and reread the fascinating literature on the risk society with mainly one question in mind: *So who is excluded?* According to these macro-sociological writings, who are the objects of the processes of exclusion we are trying to ward off our sense of uneasiness with and even more importantly, why? I think it is inadequately acknowledged that although these and other authors generally refer to comparable tendencies, the outcome of their analyses is nonetheless that very different groups are excluded and separate explanations are required for each of them. Applied to criminal law, four categories can be distinguished that are condemned to longer or stricter sentences than in the past or excluded from sentences of a more inclusive nature.

Firstly there are the *serious* offenders who are sentenced to lengthy periods in prison. In literature on the risk society, this is linked to the notion of *increased punitiveness* or *populist punitiveness*, meaning that for their own electoral benefit, politicians and policy-makers go along with what they think is the general public view on crime and the response it deserves (Bottoms 1995, p. 40).[17] This greater sensitivity to public opinion on sentencing is explained by the complex combination of factors I have cited and mainly results in a more unrelenting attitude to anyone who commits a violent or sexual offense. A study was recently conducted on differences in the extent to which national authorities are inclined to give in to pressure from perceived public views on sentencing. Cavadino and Dignan (2006) draw a direct line between *populist punitiveness* and the socio-political climate in a country. The smaller the differences between various segments of a society, the shorter the sentences, at any rate the lower the number of people in prison per 100,000 inhabitants (the prison rate). This notion is also supported by the work of Finnish researcher Lappi Sappällä. A comparison of the state expenditures and population censuses of numerous countries shows that the larger the income differences, the higher the prison rate. And the higher the percentage of the gross national product spent on social services, the lower the prison rate. There is also a direct relation between the confidence people say they have in their legal system and in each other and the prison rate. According to Lappi Sappällä, the explanation for these results is not that complicated. A community of equals who care about each other's well-being is less apt to punish its members with hard sanctions than a community where there is more distance between various groups and punishment is mainly given to *the others* (Lappi-Seppälä 2010).

The second category tends to be excluded from society for longer periods of time and not because its criminal offences are so heinous, but because it is rightly or wrongly viewed as *dangerous*. Protecting society from dangerous criminals has always been

17 A distinction needs to be drawn between this and the issue of public opinion (Bottoms 1995, p. 40). Politicians and policy-makers might take the fact that the public wants longer sentences as their point of departure, but this does not necessarily mean it is true, and it usually lacks any empirical backing. For the current situation, see Elffers' inaugural lecture (2008).

grounds for legitimizing the use of sanctions, but what has changed is that the danger is now assessed more on the basis of group than individual features, and there has been a shift in the balance between false positives and false negatives (Feeley & Simon 1994, Hudson 2002). In other words, we would prefer to have someone who would not be a repeat offender in the future (although of course we can never be certain) incarcerated longer than take the risk of releasing someone who is going to commit punishable acts again. In the Netherlands as well as in most other countries in Europe, what these changes mean concretely is that someone is no longer assumed to be dangerous on the basis of a talk or talks with a psychologist or psychiatrist, but on the basis of the outcome of a list of risk factors that ideally is confirmed or corrected by the clinical opinion of an expert but often do not (Moerings 2003, Simon & Feeley 1992, Van Swaaningen 1996). The conclusion is also more easily drawn that the risk is unacceptable, as is evident for example from the greater reluctance to grant a trial leave to offenders sentenced to detention under a hospital order (DJI 2010, p. 23) and the developments I describe as regards the long stay. As a result of all these measures, someone sentenced to detention under a hospital order in 1999 spent an average of 10.2 years in detention, whereas someone sentenced to detention under a hospital order in 1990 only spent an average of 7.3 years in detention. These figures do not include the incarceration of individuals still in detention under a hospital order at the time of the calculations. Of the people who began their detention under a hospital order in 2000, less than 50% had been released in 2010 (DJI 2012, p. 27). What is more, these figures do not reflect the latest developments, so the average duration can be expected to increase if calculated for later starting moments. The figures make offenders extremely reluctant to be tested for accountability and motivate their lawyers to back them in this connection (Muis & Van der Geest 2010).

The *scapegoats*, the third category, are often mentioned in the same breath as the dangerous offenders. This is because the more dangerousness is assessed on the basis of group features, and the wider the definition of dangerousness, the more diffuse the distinction is between the ones who are rightly and who are wrongly viewed as dangerous. But there are essential differences between the sentiments behind the various types of exclusion. I refer to drug couriers and prison inmates without a Dutch residence permit as scapegoats. In my classification system, I distinguish them from the category of dangerous offenders because there are barely any individual features to explain why they are treated differently. The distinction is legitimized by a number of striking group features such as the type of offence they have committed, the country they are from, and whether or not they have a Dutch residence permit. It is also less evident that fear or the avoidance of risk are reasons for the distinction. A Durkheimian function is frequently attributed to the scapegoat mechanism. Picking out individuals or groups who do not belong, reinforces the sense of togetherness of other members of society.

The fourth category, offenders viewed as either unmotivated to change or unable to take responsibility for their behaviour, can be referred to as *the unworthy*. They are not viewed as deserving any resocializing efforts because they messed up the chances they had in the past, they aren't motivated to keep appointments or stick to agreements. Especially in the most recent plans for modernizing the prison system, this view is taken to the extreme. 'Investments such as behavioural interventions, training and activities preparing for a return to society are only to be made in prison inmates if there is a chance of success and if their motivation and/or attitude warrants them'.[18] In my opinion, this is the most striking category. Not only because nowhere outside the Netherlands have I seen such an obsessive interest in this criterion, but also because stressing the offenders' own responsibility this way goes against the idea of neurobiological and other seemingly immutable factors as the dominant explanation for criminal behaviour, a contradiction Schuyt (2011) also recently pointed out in his Konigsberger lecture, as did Barbara Hudson (2003) earlier.

Inclusion

As I have noted, the theoretical explanations for the tendency towards harder sanctions have been far more comprehensively thought out than those for the soft end of the spectrum, notwithstanding the impressive advances there as well. Isn't it odd that new kinds of sentences are constantly being introduced to improve the offender or his circumstances so he can have a better position in society, though the theoretical explanations for this are few and, as far as they are there, rarely go very deep? One explanation lies in the concept of bifurcation itself. Bifurcation is described as a strategy to compensate for longer and longer sentences for offenders who commit extremely serious crimes by developing and enforcing far less severe sanctions for offenders who commit less serious crimes (Bottoms 1977, 1995, Cavadino & Dignan 2006). Accordingly, there are economic grounds for the shorter, more inclusive sentences, which are enforced to make money and prison cells available for the most serious offenders. It is characteristic of bifurcation that simultaneously with the lengthened sentences for serious offences, the sentences for less serious offences are substantially shortened.

Another explanation is that developing sentences to be enforced outside the prison is a way of further expanding state control that does not differ essentially from the control exercised by incarceration. Foucault calls the prison an institute generated by a desire to discipline the population and monitor segments of the population threatening to

18 Letter from the State Secretary of Justice about the project Modernising the Prison System. Parliamentary Documents II 2010/2011, 29 270, nr. 52 (Letter dated 8 November 2011).

sidestep the less drastic forms of disciplining (Foucault 1975). Alternatives to prison sentences do not counteract this aim. On the contrary, in essence it is a deeper and more extensive form of state control because it now also extends to places that are normally private domain, the family, the school, or the work place (Cohen 1979, 1985, Mathiessen 1986). Stanley Cohen sees the development of alternatives to imprisonment as forerunner of *the punitive city* Foucault predicted. Simon and Feeley, who coined the term *new penology*, similarly view the emergence of sentences to be served in society as proof of their idea that the practice of sanctioning is not characterized by a desire to rehabilitate individuals who break the law, but by a wish to manage criminality effectively by detecting high risk groups and keeping them under supervision (Simon & Feeley 1992, p. 40). As the most important support for their claim that the latent functions of alternatives to imprisonment are more dominant than the overt ones, they recurrently note that the alternative nature of the sentences is not actually put into practice. Research has repeatedly demonstrated that sanction modalities presented as alternatives have a magnetic or net-widening effect, which means the alternatives are predominantly or at any rate partially utilized in cases where in the past, a less lengthy sentences or no sentence at all would have been pronounced (Simon & Feeley 1992, p. 439).

In his magnificent epos on two centuries of crime and punishment in the Netherlands, Herman Franke expresses his aversion to macro-sociological explanations of developments in the prison system, emphasizing the evil intent of members of the ruling class, who deliberately propagate the most important sanctioning changes to further their own economic interests (Franke 1990, p. 762). They have too many characteristics of conspiracy theories for his taste. Doesn't anyone believe, Franke (2007, p.23) wonders as regards the introduction of the cell system, that prison reformers and politicians were truly convinced this was the best solution to the problem of criminality? In his opinion, the stronger legal position of prison inmates and the development and enforcement of milder forms of sentencing are a direct result of the civilizing process described by Elias (1936, 2001). The need for greater compassion generated by the increasing complexity of society has also led to a greater sensitivity to the suffering of prison inmates. This same sensitivity has made it more difficult to justify inflicting suffering. In addition to inflicting suffering, retribution and deterrence, starting in the second half of the nineteenth century, improving the perpetrator was also viewed as an important justification for enforcing sanctions (Franke 2007, p. 34). This is also in keeping with Van Ruller's notion that sentencing needs to be rational; in other words, it has to contribute effectively towards combating crime (Van Ruller 1993, p. 340 ff). The civilization theory can also explain the impulse given to the use of extramural sanctions in the 1970s. It is clear from, mainly foreign research conducted during this period that the results of resocialization efforts in the prison setting were quite disappointing (Boone 2007, pp. 233-234). Oddly enough, as Franke also notes, this only put more pressure on the prison sentence (Franke 2007, p. 36). Now that different forms of sanctioning did not appear to contribute towards the improvement of the offenders undergoing them, the prison sentence itself was under pressure, and enthusiastic efforts were made to find alternatives that would serve the purpose of effective punishment.

I largely agree with Franke's views. The search for sanctions less intrusive than deprivation of liberty, primarily comes from the historical explicable desire that sanctions also have to serve positive objectives. The very fact that after all the failures, efforts are still being made to find forms of sanctioning with resocialization and reintegration as their primary aim is from a theoretical point of view just as fascinating as the hard side of bifurcation.[19] The fact that certain groups are systematically excluded from these sanctions is something I see less as the result of a conscious strategy (as Cohen sees it) than as the 'unintended effect of human strivings' (as Franke sees it, 1990, p. 761). At any rate, I think it would be worthwhile to seriously investigate the mechanisms that cause this phenomenon, a thought that will be worked out in the next session.

Micro-Level

No matter how much insight theory formation on the risk society can grant into the form the sanction implementation has come to have in the Netherlands, it is still necessary to supplement this insight with more precise observations at the micro-level. By micro-level, I mean the level of individual decision makers, and as regards the use of sanctions this can include judges, public prosecutors, parole officers as well as prison personnel. Whether or not someone is given community service or a suspended sentence or is selected for a special prison programme or a behavioural intervention is usually not stipulated by general regulations and policy but is decided by an individual official who often has ample leeway to choose whichever option he feels is most suitable. How do these officials arrive at a decision to apply an inclusive or an exclusive sanction? How do they apply the rules, and how are they influenced by the macro-sociological developments I have described? Garland himself warns that theory-based discussions on the changed penal climate should be viewed as a basis and not as a substitute for empirical analyses (Garland 1997, p. 204, Robinson 2002, p. 6). Also the observation that the processes of exclusion attributed to the altered society not always occur to the same extent (Snacken 2011), stimulates us to make more precise

19 That more and more sanction modules are constructed that only aim at incapacitation, which means that the opportunities to commit offences are restricted or excluded, without serving any other aim, proves that the continuation of this search is not evident. Malsch and Duker will publish a volume on this topic soon (Malsch & Duker 2012).

observations about the conditions processes of this kind occur under. The comparative research I am conducting with my foreign colleagues in the framework of our network subsidy financed by the European Union[20] can gain much insight, but also research comparing various organizations within one country shows that organizations can differ in the extent to which they are sensitive to pressure exerted by a hardening punitive climate.[21] Dutch research on the decision-making processes of criminal law officials has been scarce, in particular in the light of processes of inclusion and exclusion as sketched above.[22] In the more ample studies conducted abroad, I have been able to distil two other spheres of influence that influence these decision making processes, besides the macro-sociological perspective I have just described, and that is usually referred to as the *penal discourse*.[23] They pertain to the influence of the organization and organization culture, *i.e., the administrative organizational perspective*, and the complex influence that the rules and principles they are based on exert on the decision-making and its outcome, *i.e., the judicial perspective*. I would like to give three examples from my own research to illustrate these various spheres of influence.

The classical study on decision making by the staff in the field is *Street Level Bureaucracies* by Michael Lipsky. Here he describes the tension between managers and officials in the service sector such as the Welfare Department and Police Department.

20 COST (European Cooperation in Science and Technology) IS 1106, Offender Supervision in Europe.

21 A striking result of the study I conducted with Moerings on the increase in the prison rate in the Netherlands is for example that in the period from 1985 to 2005, the Public Prosecution Department exerted much more influence on the trend towards increasing exclusion than the police or the courts (Boone & Moerings 2007, also Vollaard & Molenaar 2009).

22 Concerning the related, but more restricted research on selectivity based on social class (including ethnic background), Rovers published an overview in 1999. He comes to the conclusion that most research is outdated, based on quantitative sources and has the outcome of decision making processes as a central topic (*if* selectivity exists) instead of the decision making *process* itself (Rovers 1999).

23 British and Scottish researchers in particular have conducted a good series of studies about the influence of the penal discourse, and more concretely the thinking in terms of risk and security, on the decision-making of probation officers. One instrument they use to investigate this is shadow writing, a research technique whereby the researcher also draws up a social inquiry report and is then able to have an in-depth discussion with the probation officer about the contents and differences between the two reports (Halliday *et al.* 2008). Their general conclusion is that risk, even in a quantitative sense, only plays a marginal role in the formulation of social inquiry reports to be presented to the judge. In so far as risk assessment serves as the basis for a recommendation, a high risk of recidivism can serve as an argument *against* as well as an argument *for* a rehabilitation intervention. In the former case, the reasoning is that a sentence served in society is too much of a safety risk, and in the latter case, that a rehabilitation intervention is a necessary prerequisite to reduce the risk of recidivism. The researchers conclude that probation officers still try to arrive at a professional evaluation of how changeable or how incorrigible the offender is going to be. Although the terminology used to formulate this conclusion has been modernized, it still refers to the traditional task of selecting which offenders are to be excluded from the more lenient approach (McNeill *et al.* 2009, p. 429). This selection is however not purely or predominantly made on the basis of statistical considerations (Robinson 2002, pp. 16, 17). Marjolein Huizinga also arrives at this conclusion in her recently completed thesis on how probation officers arrive at their selection-related decisions and the role of the responsiveness principle in this connection (Huizinga 2011).

Managers give priority to quantitative aspects, but the officials are more interested in giving their clients better quality. To cope with this constant dilemma, the officials opt for adaptation strategies, such as creaming or the selection of clients. In the process, their preference is usually for clients with the best chance of success in terms of the organisation. In my 2007 study on the accessibility and quality of rehabilitation work for ethnic minority clients, I came across numerous instances of creaming (Boone 2002). It is often at the expense of ethnic minority clients, and not because of their different ethnic background but because they more frequently exhibit features that make them a more problematic target group for rehabilitation services than other clients. Their mastery of the Dutch language is often poor or non-existent, they more frequently deny committing the offence they are accused of, and it is not as easy to motivate them to adjust to Dutch society. The high production pressure at the time in the Probation Office made it difficult to generate good opportunities for rehabilitation. Suspects were not visited and given early assistance at the police station because they, according to telephonic information by the police, either did not speak the language or denied committing the offence. Substantially fewer social inquiry reports were written, and the reports that were filed more frequently failed to consult anyone from the offender's circle of acquaintances, friends and relatives, although this was recognised as an important aspect of good quality of the reports.[24] Lipsky's magnum opus was widely praised, but there were also numerous corrections and additions.[25] If only because of the transformation of various agencies in the field of criminal law to output-steered organizations, I feel the study of the decision-making at these agencies should not be viewed as having lost any of its significance.

Rules and guidelines designed to restrict the free discretionary power of criminal law officials are often defended by referring to the need to expand formal equality before the law. Research in the sociology of law demonstrates that an excessive emphasis on formal equality before the law can actually increase material legal inequality and reinforce social inequality (Boone 2004; Boone & Korf 2010). Sentencing guidelines can have this effect. After all, agreements can only be made about what can be measured and quantified, and uniformity based on the wrong grounds can contribute just as much to legal inequality as unfounded differences (Loth 2001, p. 111). Using the weight of transported drugs as a point of departure when trying drug smugglers would

24 The most interesting research result is that there were also probation officers who absolutely refused to engage in cherry picking. They made every effort to also reach the least accessible group of clients and provide rehabilitation activities without it being at the expense of their total production. Just as Lipsky predicts, they were not rewarded for their extra efforts by the agencies they worked for.

25 For example, Evans notes that Lipsky has an overly one-dimensional view of the relation between managers and staff in the field and points out the forgotten role of professionalism in his analysis (Evans 2011). Halliday *et al.* note the importance of working inter-professionally (the chain approach) on theory formation regarding street level bureaucracies (Halliday *et al.* 2009).

seem to be an excellent example of this danger. The study I conducted in 2004 on the use of sentencing guidelines when trying cocaine smugglers shows that the presiding judges trying drug couriers arrested at Amsterdam Airport Schiphol also feel the sentencing guidelines they themselves formulated lead to outcomes that are overly rigid (Boone 2004). However, proposals for making the guidelines more flexible and allowing more leeway for considering individual factors were not immediately welcomed by all the judges. The production pressure was high at the time due to the deluge of cocaine smugglers that organized crime was sending to the airport and the strict guidelines made it easier for them to cope efficiently with the huge inflow of cases. The quantitative testing I conducted with Dirk Korf of the hypotheses based on this study shows that in a substantial number of cases, the judges still deviated from the guidelines. However, the testing also confirms that guidelines can contribute towards enlarging social legal inequality. Judges deviate from the guidelines in a downward direction twice as frequently for suspects born in the Netherlands as for suspects born abroad (Boone & Korf 2010).

In criminal law and sentencing law, there is a built-in resistance against excessive use or otherwise disproportional sentencing. There are for example the culpability principle, the principle of last resort, and the principle of minimal restrictions, all of which essentially mean the administration of criminal law, and in particular sentences, should be applied with moderation. Decision making on the part of criminal law officials occurs in the field of tension between the resistance built into criminal law, the upward pressure exerted on criminal law by the developments in the penal climate I describe, and the efficiency demands made by the organization. These efficiency demands are visible for example in a study I conducted with my colleagues in Utrecht on the extent to which judges use their legal authority to exert influence on the enforcement of sanctions. We observed court sessions and then asked the judges about their underlying reasons for the decisions they made. One of the findings is that there are important aspects of the judges' authority that they structurally fail to put into effect with the argument that they do not want to get in the way of other participants in the process whom they hesitantly refer to as *partners in the chain*. Although they are convinced in some cases that a suspended sentence under the supervision of a probation officer would be more appropriate than a prison sentence, if no such proposal is submitted by the Probation Service, this is not the decision they make. After all, the Probation Service does not want to be stuck with any *unexpected gifts*, in other words, cases where they themselves have not made a positive recommendation. The judges also go along with *agreements* made between the Public Prosecution Department and Probation Office about the kind of cases that are referred on for advisory reports or pre-sentence reports concerning the suspect. As a consequence, the judges automatically adopt the exclusion factors adhered to by the Probation Office and Public Prosecution Department. This procedure gives rise to certain questions regarding the sentencing freedom and independence of the judges and the principle of individualized sentencing (Boone *et al.* 2009).

Those who take re-socialization, behavioural change or even just diminishing recidivism as an important aim, and actual policy points to that in my opinion, should worry about the categorical exclusion of certain groups of offenders, as mentioned above. The question of how penal officers reach their decision and under what circumstances this leads to (breaching) an inclusive or an exclusive sanction should be a topic of systematic research. Large-scale quantitative research concerning the outcomes of decision-making processes will lead to a reproduction of the data we know by now. Qualitative and ethnographic research on how decision making takes place can clarify what hinders the imposition or continuation of an inclusive sanction and under what circumstances these hindrances can be overcome, also for the categories of offenders I mentioned earlier.

Normative Evaluation

This brings me to the last two questions I would like to address in this inaugural lecture. Should bifurcation be viewed as something undesirable? And if so, is there anything we can do about it? To start with the first question, there would seem to be a certain logic to the fact that the most severe sentences are reserved for the worst or most dangerous offenders, and the more lenient and more inclusive sanctions are used for less dangerous and serious offenders. Bottoms, who coined the term bifurcation, also acknowledges this.[26] In the Netherlands, Van Stokkom views a policy that reserves long sentences for serious and repeat offenders and short ones for occasional criminals in principle as a form of pragmatic sanction policy (Van Stokkom 1999, p. 42). I have just tried to show that the line between hard and soft sentencing definitely does not run parallel to the one between serious and less serious offenders, and not even to the one between dangerous and less dangerous perpetrators, as the theory around the risk society would seem to suggest. The explanation for the enforcement of exclusive or inclusive sanctions should be sought instead in the force of worldwide societal exclusion processes regarding certain groups and the mechanism of giving more privileged perpetrators priority above less privileged ones. There are practical as well as judicial arguments to be presented against this practice.

As regards the practical objection: In this inaugural lecture I not only wish to emphasize the hardening of the penal climate, I also want to show that at the same time, one

26 But as Bottoms notes as far back as 1977, 'if this bifurcation is to be the keystone of future policy, it only raises all the more starkly the problem as to what and who are to be deemed to be "grave crimes" and "serious offenders". And there is at present no hint of any adequate theoretical justification in this area' (Bottoms 1977, p. 91).

new initiative after the other has been taken to develop penal interventions that have a positive effect on the conduct of the offender and improve his or her position in society. It is nonetheless quite illogical and counter-productive for research to repeatedly show that sanctions primarily enforced to prevent recidivism are predominantly used for precisely those offenders who need them the least. It is just as counter-productive, if not immoral, not to provide foreign prison inmates with Dutch lessons or activities that can prepare them to return to whatever society they will be returning to just because they will have to leave the Netherlands after their release. After all, research does repeatedly show that a substantial percentage of them will ultimately be remaining in the Netherlands and the Dutch Supreme Court abandoned this line of reasoning as far back as 1987 (Boone & Kox 2012).

Any number of judicial objections can be and actually have been put forward against some of the excrescences of the sanction enforcement I have described. 'To do justice to the ultra-other, we need to put rights at the centre of our models of justice', Hudson rightly notes (Hudson 2003, p. 213). Snacken also calls for the introduction of human rights instruments to arrive at a more reductionist criminal law policy (Snacken 2010, p. 275). In the right to resocialization, I have discovered a comprehensive argument against the form bifurcation has assumed in the Netherlands. Although such a right is often discussed, it can be easily derived from Section 10, Subsection 3, of the International Covenant on Political and Civil Rights, a Section the Netherlands didn't make a restriction to.[27] In the Netherlands, resocialization is primarily approached as an aim of the implementation of sentencing. This approach quickly turns the notion that this aim should be abolished or revised for certain groups if it is not adequately achieved into a legitimate line of reasoning. However I have not gone on and on about inclusive sanctions because I necessarily believe they make a substantial contribution towards reducing recidivism, the narrow interpretation usually given of the resocialization aim. The success rates are usually modest[28] and this is not surprising if we take into consideration the miserable situations many offenders are in at the time of their arrest. Apart from the effect to be achieved, I am in favour of recognizing a right to resocialization as was acknowledged by the German Federal Constitutional Court in 1973. The Court bases its recognition on the constitutionally acknowledged right to human dignity and the freedom to develop one's talents and the duty of the state to aid and assist whatever individuals in society are 'restricted in their societal development because of their personal weakness, culpability, inability or social deprivation'. The Court includes convicts and ex-convicts in this category (Morgenstern 2011, pp. 21-22). Obviously the recognition of this kind

27 Thanks to Gerard de Jonge.
28 Hermanns (2009) cites a reduction in recidivism of 8.2% for the most successful interventions.

of right does not solve the problems entailed in actually putting it into effect, but it does mean these individuals cannot simply be excluded from resocialization efforts based on the argument that they do not belong to a certain target group or are felt to have forfeited their chances.

In Closing

The last question I posed is *Is there anything we can do about it?* I am a university researcher and universities are in difficult financial straits nowadays, so my answer is obvious: more research. With my students, junior researchers, future PhD students and colleagues in the Netherlands and abroad, I hope to conduct more research in the years to come into the processes of inclusion and exclusion along the lines that have been stipulated. I also hope to be able to examine the phenomena that seemingly contradict the tendencies I have sketched, because I have not been able to get to them in the past half hour.

A Few Words of Gratitude

The University of Groningen protocol prohibits expressing words of thanks at the end of an inaugural lecture, as is customary at all the other universities. I asked why this is the case. It turned out that in the past, newly appointed professors knew no bounds in their lengthy words of gratitude, and the point is to prevent this from happening in the future. I totally endorse this aim, which is why I will keep my gratitude short. I would like to thank the University of Groningen administration for the confidence it had in me. Berend Keulen for his invitation to apply for a position in Groningen. Esther Gerringa and Martina Althoff for the mental and physical support in preparing this day. Dina Siegel and Francois Kristen for the warm-hearted and uncomplicated way they welcomed and facilitated my appointment. Constantijn Kelk, once again you haven't allowed your health to keep you from attending an important day in my career. I am proud to have completed my dissertation under your supervision. Martin Moerings, in a sense I have always continued to see you as my supervisor. Before I realized it myself, you both saw that this was the best chair for me. I would like to thank Kristel Beyens and Jolande uit Beijerse for critically reading and commenting on an earlier version of this lecture. Dear Boes. Despite you, I wrote in the foreword to my dissertation, and not everyone liked that. The fact that you were able to laugh about it made me confident that our new relationship was not going to be short-lived, but the words that were spoken at the time aren't words I would dare to repeat today. Dear Belle and Parel, of course you are the rascals who will always come first for me.

Ik heb gezegd.

References

Bauman, Z. (2000), *Liquid Modernity*, Cambridge: Polity Press.

Beck, U. (1992), *The risk society; toward a new modernity*, London: Sage.

Boone, M. & G. de Jonge (eds.) (2001), *De Penitentiaire Beginselenwet in werking, Het gevangeniswezen anno 2001*, Deventer: Gouda Quint.

Boone, M. (2002), *Leren diversifiëren. Reclassering en culturele diversiteit*, Utrecht: Willem Pompe Institute.

Boone, M. (2003), Penitentiaire beginselen en de bewaring van vreemdelingen, *PROCES*, 82(6), pp. 301-312.

Boone, M. (2004), Richtlijn of regel? De rechterlijke macht en de bolletjesslikkers, in: M. Boone, R.S.B. Kool, C.M. Pelser & T. Boekhout van Solinge (eds.), *Discretie in het strafrecht*, The Hague: Boom Juridische Uitgevers, pp. 227-248.

Boone, M. (2006), De Noodwet Drugskoeriers als proeftuin voor een grootschalige versobering van het gevangeniswezen, *PROCES*, 85 (4), pp. 140-153.

Boone, M. (2007), Selective Rehabilitation, in: M. Boone & M. Moerings (eds.), *Dutch Prisons*, The Hague: Boom Juridische Uitgevers, pp. 231-249.

Boone, M. & M. Moerings (2007), Growing Prison Rates, in: M. Boone & M. Moerings (eds.), *Dutch Prisons*, Den Haag: Boom Juridische uitgevers, p. 51-76.

Boone, M. (2009), Er zitten hier alleen moslims. Een bijzondere afdeling voor 'terroristen': Mag het? Werkt het?, in: C. Brants & S. Van der Poel (eds.), *Diverse Kwesties, Liber amicorum prof. F. Bovenkerk*, The Hague: Boom Juridische Uitgevers, Pompe series, no. 56.

Boone, M. (2010), Only for Minor Offences, Community Service in the Netherlands, *European Journal of Probation*, 2 (1), pp. 22-40.

Boone, M., A. Beijer, A.A. Franken & C. Kelk (2009), *De tenuitvoerlegging van sancties: maatwerk door de rechter?*, The Hague: Boom Juridische Uitgevers, Pompe series, no. 53.

Boone, M. & D.J. Korf (2010), Bestraffing van cocaïnesmokkelaars. Richtlijnen, rechters, rechtbanken en de persoon van de dader, *Tijdschrift voor Criminologie,* (52) 3, pp. 239-258.

Boone, M. and M. Kox (2012), What works for irregular migrants in the Netherlands, *European Journal of Probation*, (4) 3, pp. 54-68.

Bottoms, A. (1977), Reflections on the renaissance of dangerousness, *Howard Journal of Penology and Crime Prevention,* 16, pp. 70-96.

Bottoms, A (1995), The philosophy and politics of punishment and sentencing, in: C. Clarkson& R. Morgan (eds.), *The politics of sentencing reform*, Oxford: Clarendon Press, pp. 17-19.

Boutellier, H. (2002), *De veiligheidsutopie,* The Hague: Boom Juridische Uitgevers.

Cavadino, M. & J. Dignan (2006), *Penal systems. A comparative approach,* London: Sage.
Cohen, S. (1979), The punitive city: notes on the dispersal of social control, *Contemporary Crises*, 3 (4), pp. 341-363.
Cohen, S. (1985), Visions of social control: crime, punishment and classification, Cambridge: Polity Press.
Dienst Justitiële Inrichtingen (2010), Tbs in getal, 2005-2009
Dienst Justitiële Inrichtingen (2011a), *Gevangeniswezen in getal 2005-2010.*
Dienst Justitiële Inrichtingen (2011b), *Tbs in getal 2005-2010.*
Dienst Justitiële Inrichtingen (2011c), *Vreemdelingenbewaring in getal.*
Dienst Justitiële Inrichtingen (2012), *Forensische zorg in getal, 2007-2011.*
Downes, D. & R. van Swaaningen (2007), The Road to Dystopia? Changes in the Penal Climate of the Netherlands, in: M. Tonry & C. Bijleveld (eds.), Crime and Justice in the Netherlands. Volume 35, Chicago: The University of Chicago Press, pp. 31-71
Elffers, H. (2008), *Een straffe aanpak,* The Hague: Boom Juridische Uitgevers.
Elias, N. (1936/1980), *Über den Prozeß der Zivilisation Soziogenetische und psychogenetische Untersuchungen. Erster Band: Wandlungen des Verhaltens in den weltlichen Obersichten des Abendlandes.* Frankfurt am Main: Suhrkamp.
Elias, N. (2001), *Het civilisatieproces. Sociogenetische en psychogenetische onderzoekingen,* Amsterdam: Uitgeverij Boom.
Evans, T. (2011), Professionals, managers and discretion, critiquing street level bureaucracy, *British Journal of Social Work,* 41, pp. 368-386.
Feeley, M. & J. Simon (1994), Actuarial justice: the emerging new criminal law, in: Nelken, D. (ed.), *The futures of criminology,* London: Sage, pp. 173-201.
Fischer, T., M. Captein & B. Zwirs (2012), *Gedragsinterventies voor volwassen justitiabelen. Stand van zaken en mogelijkheden voor innovatie,* The Hague: Boom Juridische uitgevers, WODC Research and Policy, no. 302.
Fiselier, J. (1998), Lang leve de reclassering, *Sancties,* vol. 4, pp. 205-209.
Forum Levenslang (June 2010), *Factsheet. Feitelijke gegevens over de levenslange gevangenisstraf.*
Forum Levenslang (July 2011), *Update Factsheet. Feitelijke gegevens over de levenslange gevangenisstraf.*
Foucault, M. (1975), *Surveiller et punir. Naissance de la prison.* France: Gallimard.
Franke, H. (1990), *Twee eeuwen gevangen: misdaad en straf in Nederland.* Utrecht: Het Spectrum.
Franke, H. (2007), Two centuries of imprisonment: socio-historical explanations, in: M. Boone & M. Moerings (eds.), *Dutch prisons,* The Hague: Boom Juridische uitgevers, pp. 5-51.
Garland, D. (1997), Governmentality and the problem of crime: Foucault, criminology, sociology, *Theoretical Criminology,* 1 (2), pp. 173-214.

Garland, D. (2001), *The culture of control. Crime and social order in contemporary society*, Oxford: The University of Chicago Press.
Giddens, A. (1990), *The consequences of modernity*, Cambridge: Polity Press.
Halliday, S., N. Burns, N. Hutton, F. McNeil & C. Tata (2008), Shadow writing and participant observation: a study of criminal justice social aork around sentencing, *Journal of Law and Society*, 35 (2), pp. 189-213.
Halliday, S., N. Burns, N. Hutton, F. McNeill & C. Tata (2009), Street-level bureaucracy, interprofessional relations and coping mechanisms: a study of criminal justice social workers in the sentencing process, *Law & Policy*, 32 (4), pp. 405-427.
Hermanns, J. (2009), Nieuwe wegen in het terugdringen van recidive?, *PROCES*, (88) 3, pp. 147-154.
Hudson, B. (2002), Punishment and Control, in: M. Maguire, R. Morgan & R. Reiner (eds.), *The Oxford handbook of criminology* (third edition), Oxford: Oxford University Press, pp. 231-254.
Hudson, B. (2003), *Justice in the risk society, challenging and re-affirming justice in late modernity*, Sage: London.
Huizinga, M. (2011), *Totstandkoming van een adviesrapportage door reclasseringswerkers*, Master's thesis in Criminology, University of Utrecht.
Inspectie voor sanctietoepassing (2006), *Praktijk penitentiaire programma*, Inspectierapport Themaonderzoek.
Inspectie voor sanctietoepassing (2008), *Praktijk penitentiaire programma's*, Inspectiebericht, Vervolgonderzoek.
N. Jörg, Kelk, C. & A.H. Klip (2012), Strafrecht met mate, Deventer: Kluwer (12th druk).
Kalidien, S. & N. de Heer-de Lange (eds.) (2011), *Criminaliteit en rechtshandhaving 2010. Ontwikkelingen en samenhangen*, The Hague: Boom Juridische uitgevers.
Kalmthout, A.M. van (2007), Het regiem van de vreemdelingenbewaring; de balans na 25 jaar, *Justitiële Verkenningen*, 33 (4), pp. 89-102.
Kelk, C. (1998), De reclassering van gedetineerden, *Delikt en Delinkwent*, 28 (5), pp. 421-426.
Lappi-Seppäla, J. (2010), Finnland, in: F. Dünkel *et al.* (eds.), *Kriminalität, Kriminalpolitik, strafrechtliche Sanktionspraxis und Gefangenraten im europäischen Vergleich*, Mönchengladbach: Forum Verlag Godesberg, pp. 325-392.
Lipsky, M. (1980), *Street-level bureaucracies: dilemmas of the individual in public services*, New York: Russell Sage Foundation.
Loth, M. A. (2001), Rechterlijke samenwerking en rechtsvinding, in: C.P.M. Cleiren & G.K. Schoep (eds.), *Rechterlijke samenwerking*, Deventer: Gouda Quint, E.M. Meijers Institute, pp. 111-120.
Lünneman, K., G. Bijers & M. Wentink (2005), *Werkstraffen: succes verzekerd? Succes- en faalfactoren bij werkstraffen van meerderjarigen*. Utrecht: Verweij-Jonker Instituut.

Malsch, M. & M. Duker (eds.), *Incapacitation Trends and Perspectives.* Ashgate Publishing LTD.

Mathiessen, T. (1986), The politics of abolition, *Contemporary Crises*, 10 (1), pp. 81-94.

McNeill, F., N. Burns, S. Halliday, N. Hutton & C. Tata (2009), Risk, responsibility and reconfiguration: Penal adaptation and misadaptation, *Punishment and Society*, 11 (4), pp. 419-442.

Moerings, M. (2003), Straffen met het oog op veiligheid, een onderneming vol risico's, inaugural lecture, University of Leiden.

Morgenstern, C. (2011), Judicial rehabilitation in Germany: the use of criminal records and the removal of recorded convictions, *European Journal of Probation*, 3 (1), pp. 20-35.

Muis, K. P. M. A. & L. van der Geest (2010), *TBS uit de gratie*, Utrecht: Nyfer.

Nelissen, P.Ph. (2001), Kansarme en kansrijke gedetineerden, selectiviteit en tweedeling in penitentiaire inrichtingen, *Justitiële Verkenningen*, 27 (6), pp. 66-76.

Poort, R. (2009), *Fundamenten voor toezicht. Over de grondslagen voor de ontwikkeling van reclasseringstoezicht,* Utrecht: Reclassering Nederland, Stichting Verslavingsreclassering ggz, Leger des Heils.

Pratt, J. (2005), Elias, punishment and decivilization, in: J. Pratt *et al.* (eds.), *The new punitiveness, trends, theories, perspectives*, Cullompton: Willan Publishing.

Raad voor Strafrechtstoepassing en Jeugdbescherming (2007), *Advies: De zorg aan gedetineerden met een ernstige psychische stoornis of verslaving.*

Raad voor Strafrechtstoepassing en Jeugdbescherming (2008a), *Advies: Gedetineerden met een verstandelijke beperking.*

Raad voor Strafrechtstoepassing en Jeugdbescherming (2008b), *Advies: Long Stay.*

Raad voor Strafrechtstoepassing en Jeugdbescherming (2010), *Advies: Regimesontwikkeling in inrichtingen voor strafrechtelijk veroordeelde vreemdelingen.*

Raad voor Strafrechtstoepassing en Jeugdbescherming (2011), *Advies: Minimumstraffen voor recidive bij zware minimumstraffen.*

Reidnied, J. (2001), De doelgroep en doelstelling van het penitentiair programma, in: M. Boone & G. de Jonge (eds.), *De Penitentiaire Beginselenwet in werking*, Pompe series, vol. 35, Deventer: Gouda Quint, pp. 35-59.

Robinson, G. (2002), Exploring risk management in probation practice: Contemporary developments in England and Wales, *Punishment and Society*, 4 (5), pp. 5-24.

Rovers, B. (1999), *Klassenjustitie, overzicht van onderzoek naar selectiviteit in de Nederlandse strafrechtsketen*, Rotterdam: Erasmus University.

Ruller, S. van (1993), Het irrationele van strafrechtelijke sancties, *Tijdschrift voor Criminologie*, 35 (4), pp. 336-350.

Sackers, H.J.B. (2011), De afschaffing van de Terroristenafdeling, *Sancties*, 6, pp. 333-337.

Schuyt, C.J.M. (2011), *Universitair verzet (1940-1945), maatschappelijk verzet en de waarde van de wetenschap: een drieluik*, Koningsberger-lezing, Universiteit Utrecht, The Hague: Boom Lemma.
Simon, J. & M. M. Feeley (1992), The new penology: notes on the emerging strategy of corrections and its implications, *Criminology*, 30 (4), pp. 449-474.
Snacken, S. (2010), Resisting punitiveness in Europe, *Theoretical Criminology*, 14 (273), pp. 273-291.
Snacken, S. (2011), Conclusion: why and how to resist punitiveness in Europe, in: S. Snacken & E. Dumortier (eds.), *Resisting punitiveness in Europe? Welfare, human rights and democracy*, London and New York: Routledge, pp. 247-260.
Stokkom, B.A.M. van (1999), Pragmatisch sanctiebeleid. Zacht waar het kan, hard waar het moet, *Justitiële Verkenningen*, 25 (6), pp. 41-56.
Swaaningen, R. van (1996), Justitie als verzekeringsmaatschappij, *Justitiële Verkenningen*, 22 (5), pp. 82-97.
Tonry, M. (ed.) (2007), Crime, punishment and politics in comparative perspective, *Crime and Justice. A Review of Research*, vol. 36, Chicago: University Press.
Tulder, F. van (2011), De straffende rechter, *Nederlands Juristenblad*, 24, pp. 1544-1550.
Tulkens, H.J.J. (1988), *Graden van vrijheid*, Arnhem: Gouda Quint.
Veldhuis, T.M. *et al.* (2010), *Terroristen in Detentie. Evaluatie van de Terroristenafdeling*, University of Groningen, Department of Behavioural and Social Sciences.
Verhagen, J. (2011), *Gedetineerden ontmaskerd. Hoe in Nederland over gedetineerden wordt gedacht en hoe het werkelijk 'zit'*, Veenhuizen: Nationaal Gevangenismuseum.
Vollaard, B.A. & D.E.G. Molenaar (2009), Beperkte invloed rechter op gebruik celstraf, *Nederlands Juristenblad*, pp. 1208-1215.
Wermink, H., A. Blokland, P. Nieuwbeerta & N. Tollenaar (2009), Recidive na werkstraffen en na gevangenisstraffen. Een gematchte vergelijking, *Tijdschrift voor Criminologie*, 51 (3), pp. 211-228.
Wermink, H., J. de Keijser & P. Schuyt (2012), Verschillen in straftoemeting in soortgelijke zaken. Een kwantitatief onderzoek naar de rol van specifieke kenmerken van de dader, *Nederlands Juristenblad*, (86) 11, pp. 727-733.
Wingerden, S. G. C. van & P. Nieuwbeerta (2006), Ontwikkelingen in de lengte van gevangenisstraffen voor moord en doodslag: een trend naar langere straffen. *Trema Tijdschrift voor de Rechterlijke Macht*, 29 (8), pp. 329-337.
Young, J. (1999), *The exclusive society: Social exclusion, crime, and difference in late modernity*, London: Sage Publications.

Eigen boeven eerst

Eigen boeven eerst

Insluiting en uitsluiting in de sanctietoepassing

Rede uitgesproken bij de aanvaarding
van het ambt van hoogleraar
Penologie en Penitentiair recht aan
de Rijksuniversiteit Groningen op 21 februari 2012

door

prof. dr. M.M. Boone

eleven
international publishing

Published, sold and distributed by Eleven International Publishing
P.O. Box 85576
2508 CG The Hague
The Netherlands
Tel.: +31 70 33 070 33
Fax: +31 70 33 070 30
e-mail: sales@budh.nl
www.elevenpub.com

Sold and distributed in USA and Canada
International Specialized Book Services
920 NE 58th Avenue, Suite 300
Portland, OR 97213-3786, USA
Tel: 1-800-944-6190 (toll-free)
Fax: +1 503 280-8832
orders@isbs.com
www.isbs.com

Eleven International Publishing is an imprint of Boom uitgevers Den Haag.

ISBN 978-94-90947-96-5

Cover image: Constant, Labyrismen 11, 1968.

Printed in The Netherlands

Inhoud

Mijnheer de Rector Magnificus, zeer geachte aanwezigen,

In 2011 is een wetsvoorstel bij de Tweede Kamer ingediend om minimumstraffen in te voeren bij recidive van de meest ernstige delicten. In zijn reactie op dit – dan nog – conceptwetsvoorstel wijst de Raad voor Strafrechtstoepassing erop dat het principe om gedetineerden te resocialiseren in het voorstel niet is terug te vinden. Voor de beoogde ('zware') groep van recidivisten wordt door het voorstel eerst en vooral voorzien in langere opsluiting. De Raad noemt dit opmerkelijk, omdat het justitiebeleid op andere fronten juist sterk op resocialisatie is gericht (RSJ 2011, p. 2).

De Raad wijst op een typisch voorbeeld van wat Cavadino en Dignan in hun invloedrijke rechtsvergelijkende studie naar sanctiesystemen in de hele wereld *bifurcation* noemen, de strategie waarbij lichte vormen van straffen worden ontwikkeld en toegepast op plegers van lichte delicten, terwijl nieuwe, extra zware straffen worden ontwikkeld voor groepen daders die geacht worden extra slecht of gevaarlijk te zijn (Cavadino & Dignan 2006, o.a. p. 82). Zij identificeren Nederland als een land waar dit verschijnsel ver is doorgedrongen. Hoewel ze op basis van de politieke ontwikkelingen in Nederland zouden verwachten dat Nederland in zijn geheel is opgeschoven van een humane en inclusieve strategie naar een meer harde en uitsluitende strategie van sanctietoepassing, is dat niet wat er is gebeurd, zo stellen zij. 'What has happened has been more like a redrawing of the boundaries of the community – to exclude those offenders who are seen like incorrigible lost souls, but still to include less serious (....) offenders' (Cavadino & Dignan 2006, p. 120-121). In deze rede wil ik langer stilstaan bij dit verschijnsel van insluiting en uitsluiting en dan vooral met betrekking tot de Nederlandse situatie. Ik zal laten zien dat er weliswaar sprake is van een tweedeling bij de toepassing van sancties, maar dat die zich niet uitsluitend of hoofdzakelijk heeft gemanifesteerd langs de lijn van ernstige en minder ernstige of gevaarlijke delictplegers. Ik zal proberen een verklaring te geven voor de vorm die *bifurcation* in de Nederlandse sanctietoepassing heeft aangenomen, zowel op een macrosociologisch niveau als vanuit een microperspectief, en ik zal daar een normatief oordeel over geven op basis van juridische principes voor de toepassing van straf. Mijn verhaal is uitsluitend gebaseerd op sanctietoepassing voor volwassen delictplegers.

Harde en zachte straffen

In plaats van over harde en zachte straffen spreken Cavadino en Dignan ook wel over insluitende en uitsluitende straffen. Insluitend zijn straffen die proberen delictplegers in de samenleving te houden of ze daarin weer een plek te geven door middel van re-integrerende activiteiten. Uitsluitend zijn straffen die delictplegers afhouden van deelname aan de samenleving en die ook niet gericht zijn op een voorbereiding van de terugkeer naar die samenleving. Nu blinkt deze tweedeling niet uit in helderheid,

maar voor mijn betoog heb ik een hele precieze indeling ook niet nodig. Duidelijk is dat Nederland de afgelopen decennia naar beide kanten verder gedifferentieerd is, om te beginnen naar de zware kant.

Hoewel het totale aantal gedetineerden in Nederland sinds een aantal jaren afneemt, is de gemiddelde duur van de straffen die worden opgelegd voor wat als de zwaarste delicten worden beschouwd, in dezelfde periode substantieel gestegen.[1] Voor geweldsdelicten rekende Van Tulder uit dat sinds 2000 20% zwaarder gestraft wordt (Van Tulder 2011, p. 1545).[2] Voor verkrachting en overige seksuele misdrijven steeg de gemiddelde straf tussen 2000 en 2009 met bijna 40% (Van Tulder 2011, p. 1545). Aparte vermelding verdient de toename van het aantal levenslang gestraften. Waar tussen 1970 en 1990 drie personen onherroepelijk tot een levenslange gevangenisstraf werden veroordeeld, gebeurde dat van 1990 tot en met juli 2011 29 keer, waarvan maar liefst 22 keer in de laatste tien jaar (Forum Levenslang, juli 2011). De levenslange straf is bovendien beduidend in zwaarte toegenomen sinds het beleid dat een levenslange gevangenisstraf – indien mogelijk – beëindigd wordt door gratie, als uitgangspunt is verlaten (Forum Levenslang, juni 2010, p. 3).

Ook voor niet-toerekeningsvatbare delictplegers is een voorziening gecreëerd die erop gericht is hen langer vast te houden. In 1999 is de eerste longstay-afdeling geopend voor tbs'ers die als onbehandelbaar worden beschouwd. Waar tbs-gestelden eerst pas op de longstay-afdeling konden worden geplaatst als ze ten minste zes jaar intramuraal waren behandeld (RSJ 2008b, p. 57), kan men nu al voor selectie voor een longstay-afdeling worden voorgedragen als de betrokkene conform de huidige stand van zaken 'alle behandelmogelijkheden heeft ondergaan' (RSJ 2008b, p. 61). Het aantal tbs-gestelden dat inmiddels op een longstay-afdeling verblijft, is sinds de opening in 1999 vertienvoudigd, van 21 plaatsen (RSJ 2008b, p. 15) naar 200 in 2010 (DJI 2011b, p. 19).

Typerend voor een proces van *bifurcation* is ook dat er aparte regimes worden gecreëerd voor die categorieën daders die als de meest zware of gevaarlijke worden beschouwd. Cavadino en Dignan noemen de extra beveiligde inrichting in Vught als een typisch voorbeeld van de Nederlandse *bifurcation*-strategie. Deze inrichting is bedoeld voor gedetineerden die als vluchtgevaarlijk worden beschouwd, ofwel omdat ze daadwerkelijk de intentie hebben gedemonstreerd om te ontsnappen, ofwel omdat ontsnappen enorm veel maatschappelijke onrust met zich zou brengen, de zogenoemde

1 Kalidien & De Heer-de Lange (2011), tabel 6.16, bijvoorbeeld gemiddeld opgelegde straf voor misdrijven tegen het leven van 695 naar 890 dagen.

2 De gemiddelde duur van de opgelegde onvoorwaardelijke gevangenisstraf voor moord en doodslag steeg tussen 1993 en 2004 van 6,3 naar 8,9 jaar (Van Wingerden & Nieuwbeerta 2006, p. 33).

maatschappelijk vluchtgevaarlijken.[3] Om ontsnapping te voorkomen is een regime gecreëerd dat zij 'unprecedented strict' noemen (Cavadino & Dignan 2006, p. 126), niet alleen in de Nederlandse context, maar ook in internationaal verband. Onder andere mogen activiteiten alleen worden ondernomen in groepjes van maximaal twee, mag bezoek alleen achter glas worden ontvangen en kunnen gedetineerden veelvuldig worden geboeid en tot in hun bilnaad worden onderzocht op de aanwezigheid van contrabande.

In deze categorie past ook de terroristenafdeling, bedoeld voor verdachten en veroordeelden van terroristische misdrijven. De terroristenafdeling werd in 2005 geopend om te voorkomen dat deze categorie gedetineerden hun radicale gedachtegoed zouden verspreiden onder andere gedetineerden. Daartoe werden zij niet alleen geïsoleerd van gedetineerden die niet met terrorisme in verband werden gebracht, maar ook onderworpen aan een zeer beperkt regime, waarin zij de weinige activiteiten die werden georganiseerd, meestal alleen moesten ondernemen. Voorzieningen voor detentiefasering en resocialisatie ontbraken. Na een zeer kritische evaluatie is de terroristenafdeling op dit moment feitelijk ongebruikt (Boone 2009; Veldhuis et al. 2010; Sackers 2011).

Kan voor de lange straffen en de bovengenoemde regimes nog worden verdedigd dat ze zijn bedoeld voor de delinquenten die de meest ernstige delicten hebben begaan, dat geldt zeker niet voor een aantal andere regimes die zich kenmerken door soberheid en het ontbreken van activiteiten die gericht zijn op het terugkeren naar de/een samenleving. Dat geldt bijvoorbeeld voor de detentiecentra die in 2002 in alle haast zijn opgericht naar aanleiding van de massale toestroom van drugskoeriers op de luchthaven Schiphol. Anders dan tot dan toe gebruikelijk was, werden drugskoeriers gedetineerd met meer personen op één cel. Ook het regime week in tal van opzichten af van het reguliere. Zo waren er geen mogelijkheden tot sport, opleiding, bibliotheekbezoek of maatschappelijke re-integratie (Boone 2006). Inmiddels worden de detentiecentra vooral bevolkt door vreemdelingen die in afwachting van hun uitzetting worden gedetineerd, en delictplegers die na afloop van hun straf het land moeten verlaten.

Voor die laatste categorie is in 2008 een afzonderlijk regime in het leven geroepen, het zogenoemde VRIS-regime. Het is bedoeld voor gedetineerden die na afloop van de opgelegde gevangenisstraf geen rechtmatig verblijf in Nederland hebben.[4] De argumentatie voor het afzonderlijk detineren van deze groep is dat resocialisatie na afloop van de straf niet aan de orde zou zijn, evenals daaraan verwante zaken als verlof,

3 Art. 6 Regeling selectie, plaatsing en overplaatsing van gedetineerden van 15 augustus 2000, nr. 5042803/00/DJI, Stcrt 2000, 176, laatstelijk gewijzigd bij Regeling van 27-7-2011, nr. 5672146/10/DJI, Stcrt. 2011, 14766.
4 Art. 20b Regeling selectie, plaatsing en overplaatsing van gedetineerden.

regionalisering en detentiefasering.[5] Ook voor deze groep zijn de omstandigheden waaronder ze gedetineerd wordt, aanmerkelijk soberder dan voor andere groepen gedetineerden. Er kan nauwelijks worden gedifferentieerd, en de psychische zorg blijft achter bij die in reguliere inrichtingen. Ook hier worden nauwelijks activiteiten georganiseerd en al helemaal geen activiteiten die gericht zijn op terugkeer. De stelselmatige detentie op meerpersoonscellen leidt soms tot onveilige situaties (RSJ 2010).[6]

Naar de zachte kant heeft zich echter ook een aanzienlijke differentiatie en verruiming voorgedaan. Met veel enthousiasme is in het begin van de jaren tachtig van start gegaan met het ontwikkelen van alternatieven voor de gevangenisstraf, de huidige taakstraffen. Men wilde de schadelijke effecten van de gevangenisstraf terugdringen en de resocialiserende potentie van straffen vergroten. Later kwamen daar ook andere doelstellingen bij, zoals het vergroten van de geloofwaardigheid van het justitieel apparaat (Boone 2010). Alleen al aan volwassenen werden in 2010 bijna 30.000 werkstraffen opgelegd (Kalidien & De Heer-de Lange 2011, p. 178).

De titel van de oratie van een van mijn voorgangers aan deze universiteit, professor Tulkens, luidde: 'Graden van vrijheid', waarmee hij doelde op de geleidelijke terug-gang van gedetineerden naar de samenleving (Tulkens 2011). Bij de introductie van de Penitentiaire Beginselenwet in 1999 werden in dat kader penitentiaire programma's geïntroduceerd, waarin gedetineerden, al dan niet voorzien van een elektronische enkelband, de laatste fase van hun detentie buiten de inrichting kunnen deelnemen aan een programma van activiteiten onder toezicht van de reclassering.[7]

In 2002 werd het programma Terugdringen Recidive geïntroduceerd bij de reclassering en het gevangeniswezen. Dit programma betekende een radicale omwenteling in het streven naar resocialisatie. Sinds die tijd wordt aan alle reclasseringscliënten en aan gedetineerden met een strafrestant van meer dan vier maanden onvoorwaardelijke gevangenisstraf een gestructureerde diagnose afgenomen van recidiverisico, oorzaken van criminaliteit en leerstijlen. De uitslag kan een aanleiding zijn om gedragsinterventies aan te bieden die het risico op recidive aanzienlijk moeten verkleinen en de positie van de gedetineerde in de samenleving moeten verbeteren. Dat kan zowel in de laatste fase van de detentie als in het kader van een voorwaardelijke straf of maatregel.

---

5 Deze veronderstelling is permanent onjuist, zoals al vaak naar voren is gebracht (Boone 2003; Van Kalmthout 2007). De Hoge Raad heeft al in 1987 bepaalt dat de opdracht tot resocialisatie zich niet beperkt tot degenen die na hun ontslag uit de gevangenis terugkeren in de Nederlandse samenleving (HR 16 januari 1987, NJ 1987, 405).

6 Ook Premininy tegen Rusland, Europees Hof voor de Rechten van de Mens, 10 februari 2011, European Human Right Cases 10-6-2011, afl. 6, p. 919-936, met noot M. Boone.

7 Als de visie van de demissionaire staatssecretaris van Veiligheid en Justitie op detentiefasering wordt doorgevoerd, zal het penitentiair programma binnenkort worden afgeschaft, Kamerstukken II 2010/11, 29 270, nr. 52, p. 5.

Sinds enkele jaren worden ook weer verwoede pogingen ondernomen om de korte onvoorwaardelijke gevangenisstraf te vervangen door een voorwaardelijke straf met bijzondere voorwaarden, omdat deze betere kansen biedt op gedragsbeïnvloeding.[8] Om de rechter te stimuleren vaker gebruik te maken van bijzondere voorwaarden is een wetsvoorstel aangenomen, waarin bijzondere voorwaarden wettelijk beter worden verankerd.[9] Ook is het reclasseringstoezicht op de naleving van bijzondere voorwaarden ingrijpend herzien (Poort 2009).

Bifurcation

Langs welke lijnen verloopt *bifurcation?* Wie ondergaan de insluitende en wie de uitsluitende sancties? Om die vraag te beantwoorden heb ik gegevens verzameld over de toepassingscriteria van de meeste sanctievormen, en gegevens verzameld over de kenmerken van degenen die ze ondergaan. Ik heb onder andere gelet op het gepleegde delict, de delictgeschiedenis, het geboorteland van de delictpleger en de eisen die worden gesteld aan motivatie en taal. Ik geef hier de opvallendste resultaten.

Uit het voorgaande bleek al dat de meest sobere regimes zijn gereserveerd voor delictplegers die niet in Nederland zijn geboren of er niet verblijven, de drugskoeriers en vreemdelingen die na afloop van hun straf geen verblijfsrecht in Nederland hebben. Ook van de gedetineerden die in gewone penitentiaire regimes verblijven, is bijna de helft buiten Nederland geboren, terwijl dat maar voor 12% van de Nederlandse bevolking geldt (Verhagen 2011, p. 22; DJI 2010, p. 23). Het geboorteland verklaart nog maar een deel van '*de overwhelming black colour of the Dutch prison population*', zoals Downes en Van Swaaningen (2007) het uitdrukken, omdat het percentage niet zichtbaar maakt hoe groot het aandeel gedetineerden is van wie een van de ouders in het buitenland is geboren.[10] De oververtegenwoordiging van gedetineerden afkomstig uit etnische minderheidsgroepen vormt mede de inspiratie voor de titel van deze oratie, maar maar ten dele, omdat de gevangenisbevolking in nog een aantal andere opzichten substantieel blijkt af te wijken van de gemiddelde Nederlandse bevolking. Jos Verhagen heeft recent een aantal kenmerken van gedetineerden in kaart gebracht aan de hand van het instrument dat de reclassering en het gevangeniswezen gebruiken om delictplegers te screenen, de Recidive Inschattings Schalen RISc (Verhagen

---

8 Kamerstukken II 2009/10, 32 319, nr. 3, p. 1.
9 Staatsblad 2011, nr. 615.
10 Uiteraard zijn de ongeveer 1200 vreemdelingen die in Nederlandse penitentiaire inrichtingen hun uitzetting afwachten, niet in dit percentage meegenomen. Het gaat in deze oratie tenslotte over 'boeven' en daartoe behoren vreemdelingen in vreemdelingenbewaring uitdrukkelijk niet, hoezeer de gevangenissetting waarin zij van hun vrijheid worden beroofd, ook een andere indruk wekt (DJI 2011c).

2011).[11] Ongeveer de helft van de gedetineerden wordt gekarakteriseerd als problematische drugsgebruiker (Verhagen 2011, p. 96). Slechts een op de vier gedetineerden had kort voor zijn detentie werk en een derde had gedurende zijn hele leven nog nooit gewerkt. Ook had de helft van de gedetineerden schulden die groter zijn dan ze met hun inkomen kunnen aflossen. Eerder al werd door onder andere de Gezondheidsraad vastgesteld dat ongeveer 6% van de gedetineerden aan psychotische stoornissen lijdt, 14-35% aan depressies en ongeveer de helft aan anti-persoonlijkheidsproblematiek, percentages die allemaal ver uitstijgen boven de normale prevalenties in de samenleving (RSJ 2007). Meer recent wordt onderkend dat een groot deel van de delictplegers een verstandelijke beperking heeft; voor gedetineerden wordt dat percentage geschat op 20-25% (RSJ 2008a).

Wie bevolken de zwaarst beveiligde inrichtingen? Van de achtergrond van de gedetineerden die sinds 1994 in de extra beveiligde inrichting (ebi) verbleven, weten we niet zoveel. Wel kunnen we uit de selectiecriteria afleiden dat het regime van de extra beveiligde inrichting niet per se bedoeld is voor verdachten en veroordeelden die de meest zware delicten hebben gepleegd, en daarmee dus niet voldoet aan de nogal slordige tweedeling die Cavadino en Dignan aanbrengen. Gedetineerden die de intentie hebben om te ontsnappen, hoeven immers niet degenen te zijn die de meest zware delicten hebben gepleegd, en dat geldt al helemaal niet voor degenen die alleen in de ebi worden gedetineerd omdat hun ontsnapping tot veel maatschappelijke onrust aanleiding zou geven. In onze schaduwevaluatie van de Penitentiaire Beginselenwet uit 2001 stelden De Jonge en ik al vast dat bij de beslissing of een persoon in de ebi moest worden gedetineerd of vastgehouden, een grote rol speelde of een verzoek tot uitlevering was gedaan (Boone & De Jonge 2001, p. 18).

Dankzij de zeer doorwrochte evaluatie van onderzoekers van de faculteit gedragswetenschappen van de Rijksuniversiteit Groningen weten we meer van de gedetineerden die op de terroristenafdelingen (TA's) verblijven. Op de terroristenafdelingen kunnen gedetineerden worden geplaatst die verdacht of veroordeeld zijn voor een terroristisch misdrijf of voor of tijdens hun detentie een boodschap van radicalisering verkondigen of verspreiden.[12] In de praktijk zijn er alleen gedetineerden op de afdeling geplaatst op grond van de eerste twee criteria (Veldhuis et al. 2010, p. 121). Sinds de opening van de terroristenafdeling in PI Vught in september 2006 zijn tot eind

11 Men kan serieus betwijfelen of dit een adequaat instrument is om de gedetineerdenpopulatie mee te beschrijven. Hoezeer het scoren op schalen ook wetenschappelijke objectiviteit pretendeert, uiteindelijk blijven het toch subjectieve inschattingen van reclasseringswerkers die mede de dominante morele opvattingen weerspiegelen. Ik beperk me in mijn samenvatting daarom tot die schalen die betrekkelijk objectief zijn vast te stellen en laat schalen, zoals denk- en gedragspatronen en emotioneel welzijn, buiten beschouwing.

12 Art. 20a Regeling selectie, plaatsing en overplaatsing van gedetineerden.

juni 2010[13] dertig gedetineerden op een van de twee terroristenafdelingen geplaatst (Van Veldhuis et al. 2010, p. 116). Opvallend is dat negen daarvan na korte tijd[14] wegens contra-indicaties zijn overgeplaatst naar een reguliere inrichting, terwijl dertien gedetineerden onmiddellijk na de rechterlijke uitspraak in vrijheid werden gesteld. Gemiddeld verbleven de gedetineerden negen maanden op de TA, een strafduur die niet duidt op delicten die door de strafrechter als zeer ernstig zijn beoordeeld en bovendien nog vertekend wordt door de paar gedetineerden die wel een lange strafduur op de TA ondergaan. Andere opvallende kenmerken van de op de TA gehuisveste gedetineerden betreft hun nationaliteit en geloof. Negen van de gedetineerden zijn in Nederland geboren, de overige 21 zijn afkomstig uit het buitenland, waaronder landen als Marokko, Turkije, Irak en Sri Lanka (Veldhuis et al. 2010, p. 117). De overgrote meerderheid van de gedetineerden die op de terroristenafdeling verbleven, had een moslimachtergrond (Boone 2007; Veldhuis et al. 2010, p. 133), hoewel in dezelfde periode ook niet-moslims gedetineerd zijn geweest voor terroristische activiteiten (Veldhuis et al. 2010, p. 120-121). Pas in een later stadium zijn enkele niet-moslims voor korte tijd op de TA gedetineerd geweest, maar dat was pas nadat er kritiek op de eenzijdige samenstelling van de TA-bevolking was geuit (Veldhuis et al. 2010, p. 133).

En op wie worden de straffen aan de andere kant van het spectrum, de zachte, insluitende straffen toegepast? Vaak wordt die vraag juist vanuit de andere kant benaderd, namelijk: wie worden er van de zachte straffen uitgesloten? Een terugkerend kritiekpunt is dat ze alleen worden toegepast op de meest 'kansrijke' categorieën delictplegers. Sociaal zwakke delictplegers zouden van toepassing worden uitgesloten (Kelk 1998; Nelissen 2001), evenals ongemotiveerde delictplegers (Fiselier 1998; Kelk 1998; Reidnied 2001) en delictplegers die afkomstig zijn van een etnische minderheidsgroep (Boone 2002). Delictplegers op wie insluitende sancties worden toegepast, vormen – kortom – het spiegelbeeld van de delictplegers die in een gesloten setting verblijven. Voor verschillende sancties die ik hierboven als insluitend heb getypeerd, is dat beeld in recent onderzoek bevestigd. Ik bespreek er drie.

Van taakstraffen is bekend dat zij veel vaker aan delictplegers worden opgelegd met een Nederlandse achtergrond dan aan delictplegers met een buitenlandse achtergrond. Wermink en collega's constateerden dat delictplegers aan wie een taakstraf wordt opgelegd, vijf keer zoveel kans hebben in Nederland te zijn geboren (Wermink et al. 2009) dan delictplegers die een korte gevangenisstraf opgelegd krijgen. Dezelfde groep onderzoekers kwam op basis van de observatie van 365 strafzaken bij de politierechter

13 Dit is de datum waarop de dataverzameling van het evaluatieonderzoek naar de terroristenafdeling is stopgezet (Veldhuis et al. 2010, p. 116).

14 Van Veldhuis 2010, p. 118. Zes binnen een maand, twee na een of twee dagen, een vrouwelijke gedetineerde van Vught naar De Schie en daarna naar een reguliere inrichting.

tot de conclusie dat verdachten met een Nederlands uiterlijk die ook de Nederlandse taal spraken, de minste kans hadden op een gevangenisstraf (Wermink et al. 2012). Eerder al kwam Lünneman tot de conclusie dat hoewel ook onder taakgestraften het percentage drugsverslaafden en werklozen hoger is dan onder de normale Nederlandse bevolking (Lünneman et al. 2005), dat toch een stuk lager is dan onder gedetineerden (Boone 2010).

In 2006 en 2008 heeft de Inspectie voor de sanctietoepassing themaonderzoek uitgebracht over de praktijk van penitentiaire programma's. Zij constateerde dat van de 5000 tot vrijheidsbeneming veroordeelde mannen die in 2005 voor een penitentiair programma in aanmerking kwamen, een derde hun detentie ook daadwerkelijk op deze wijze beëindigt. Dit betrof echter overwegend gedetineerden met weinig problemen die geen speciale interventies nodig hadden om een beperkt recidiverisico te vormen. Gedetineerden die problematisch gedrag hadden vertoond tijdens hun detentie, drugs hadden gebruikt of zorgbehoevend waren, werden niet voor een penitentiair programma geselecteerd. Deze moeilijke gedetineerden, die wel belang hadden bij specifieke interventies of behandelingen, werden geweerd; de benodigde programma's waren in onvoldoende mate voor hen beschikbaar of de risico's van mislukking voor deze groep werden te hoog ingeschat, aldus de Inspectie (Ist 2006, p. 33-37).[15]

Onlangs publiceerden Tamar Fischer, Miriam Captein en Barbara Zwirs van de vakgroep criminologie van de Erasmus Universiteit Rotterdam de resultaten van hun onderzoek naar exclusiefactoren bij de toepassing van gedragsinterventies aan volwassen justitiabelen (Fischer et al. 2012). Zij constateren vergelijkbare uitsluitingsfactoren als eerder de Inspectie voor de sanctietoepassing. Een ernstig gebrek aan motivatie, verslavingsproblematiek, onvoldoende verstandelijke vermogens en een onvoldoende beheersing van de Nederlandse taal zijn enkele van de relatieve uitsluitingsfactoren. Het ontbreken van een geldige verblijfsvergunning en een kort strafrestant staan altijd aan het aanbieden van een gedragsinterventie in de weg. Ieder voor zich komen de verschillende exclusiefactoren bij gemiddeld zo'n 25% van de kandidaten voor het programma Terugdringen Recidive voor. Of dat dan ook daadwerkelijk leidt tot uitsluiting van deelname aan een gedragsinterventie, is daarmee niet aangetoond.

15 Naar aanleiding van de reactie van de minister van Justitie op deze bevindingen (Kamerstukken II 2006/07, 24 587, nr. 198) is door de Inspectie voor de sanctietoepassing (Ist) een vervolgonderzoek verricht naar de vraag of de invoering van het programma Terugdringen Recidive tegemoetkomt aan de tekortkomingen die door de Ist werden geconstateerd. Dit bleek maar zeer ten dele het geval. Weliswaar constateert de Ist dat voor de groep zorgbehoevende gedetineerden de redenering dat iemand voor een penitentiair programma in aanmerking komt, terrein wint op de redenering dat iemand niet in aanmerking komt voor een penitentiair programma vanwege zijn problematiek, maar zij komt tegelijkertijd tot de conclusie dat er geen toename is van gedetineerden die ondanks geconstateerd drugsgebruik in een penitentiair programma geplaatst worden en dat de kans om in een penitentiair programma geplaatst te worden voor korter gestraften beduidend kleiner blijft dan voor langer gestraften (Ist 2008, p. 12-13).

Motivatie bijvoorbeeld blijkt in de praktijk veel minder streng als uitsluitingscriterium te worden gehanteerd dan uit de contra-indicaties voor gedragsinterventies naar voren komt. Toch gaat de reclassering er zelf van uit dat ten minste een kwart van de kandidaten die op basis van de RISc in aanmerking komt voor een gedragsinterventie, uitvalt door de aanwezigheid van exclusiefactoren.[16] Dit is met name zorgwekkend omdat uit hetzelfde onderzoek blijkt dat criminogene factoren, factoren die ten grondslag liggen aan criminaliteit en dus door interventies behandeld zouden kunnen worden, veel vaker voorkomen bij de groep die van interventies wordt uitgesloten.

Macroperspectief

Dan kom ik nu aan het verklarende deel van deze rede. Wat is de theoretische verklaring voor insluiting en uitsluiting, en waarom heeft het in Nederland de vorm aangenomen die hierboven is geschetst? Ik zal zowel een macrosociologisch als een microperspectief schetsen.

Uitsluiting

Hardere en meer uitsluitende straffen of maatregelen worden door verschillende theoretici in verband gebracht met een aantal ingrijpende wijzigingen die zich in de samenleving hebben voorgedaan. Sociologen als Ulrich Beck, Anthony Giddens, Zygmunt Bauman en Barbara Hudson hebben die veranderingen in aanstekelijke bewoordingen geschetst. Zij schetsen een samenleving waarin zich vanaf de jaren zestig grote veranderingen hebben voorgedaan. Emancipatie, grootschalige immigratie, enorme technologische vooruitgang, maar ook massacriminaliteit, nucleaire en terroristische dreiging. Het gemeenschappelijke punt in hun verklaringen is dat de grote veranderingen die de moderne samenleving met zich brengt, de voortdurende beweging, vloeibaarheid heeft Bauman het genoemd (Bauman 2000), en de ongrijpbaarheid van de risico's die daarmee samengaan, de burger onzeker maken en doet vastklampen aan datgene wat vertrouwd is. Wat vreemd is of een potentieel risico inhoudt, wordt afgewezen. Bovengenoemde auteurs spreken daarom wel afwisselend van een risicosamenleving (Beck 1992; Hudson 2003), een *exclusive society* (Young 1999), een controlecultuur (Garland 2001) of een zondeboksamenleving (Young 1999; Beck 1992. De nationale overheden maken enerzijds gebruik van die angst: zij kunnen immers stemmen winnen door te pretenderen wel oplossingen te hebben voor de ingewikkelde problemen waarmee burgers geconfronteerd worden, maar zij worden anderzijds overvraagd door de burger die risico's op zich af ziet komen, waartegen hij zich niet zelf meer kan beschermen of verzekeren (Giddens 1990,Beck 1992; Pratt 2005). Waar het strafrecht bedoeld is als ultimum remedium, een laatste middel dat

16 Gevangeniswezen en reclassering, Analyse TR, 20 oktober 2011, Concept 2.1 (interne notitie).

wordt ingezet om individuele, hardnekkige delictplegers een norm in te prenten waarover overwegend consensus bestaat, wordt het in een verdeelde en gefragmenteerde 'laatmoderne' samenleving veelvuldig ingezet om de – lang niet altijd duidelijke dominante – norm te stellen en af te dwingen bij hen die deze niet (zichtbaar) welgevallig is: van ultiem naar urgent strafrecht in de terminologie van Boutellier (Boutellier 2002).

Ik heb de fascinerende literatuur over de risicosamenleving vooral nog eens doorgenomen vanuit de vraag: wie worden er dan uitgesloten? Wie zijn volgens deze macrosociologische beschouwingen subject van die processen van uitsluiting, waarmee we onze gevoelens van onbehagen proberen te bezweren en, vooral, waarom? Mijns inziens wordt onvoldoende ingezien dat bovengenoemde en andere auteurs grosso modo wijzen op vergelijkbare tendensen, maar dat als uitkomst van hun analyse toch heel verschillende groepen worden uitgesloten en dat die groepen ieder op zich een eigen verklaring behoeven. Toegepast op het strafrecht kan worden gezegd dat vier categorieën delictplegers worden onderscheiden die langere of strengere straffen ondergaan dan voorheen, dan wel worden uitgesloten van straffen met een meer insluitend karakter. Ten eerste worden langere straffen opgelegd aan ernstige delictplegers. Deze tendens wordt in de literatuur over de risicosamenleving gekoppeld aan de notie van *increased punitiveness* of *populist punitiveness*, waarmee wordt bedoeld dat politici en beleidsmakers voor hun eigen electoraal gewin toegeven aan wat zij denken dat de algemene publieke opvatting is over criminaliteit en de reactie die daarop moet volgen (Bottoms 1995, p. 40).[17] Die grotere gevoeligheid voor de publieke opinie over straffen wordt verklaard door een complexe combinatie van factoren die hierboven al even werd geduid, en resulteert vooral in een onverbiddelijker houding ten opzichte van plegers van geweld en zedendelicten. Meer recent wordt ook onderzoek gedaan naar verschillen in de mate waarin nationale overheden geneigd zijn toe te geven aan de druk van de gepercipieerde publieke opvattingen over straf. Cavadino en Dignan leggen een directe relatie tussen *popular punitiveness* en het sociaal-politieke klimaat in een land (Cavadino & Dignan 2006). Naarmate de verschillen tussen diverse groepen in de samenleving kleiner zijn, wordt er ook minder zwaar gestraft, althans is het aantal mensen per 100.000 inwoners dat in de gevangenis wordt opgenomen (de detentieratio) lager. Die stelling wordt verder onderbouwd in het werk van de Finse onderzoeker Lappi-Seppällä. Een vergelijking van de staatsuitgaven en bevolkingsenquêtes van een groot aantal landen laat zien dat de detentieratio hoger is naarmate de inkomensverschillen groter zijn. De detentieratio is lager naarmate een groter deel van het bruto nationaal product wordt uitgegeven aan sociale voorzieningen. Ook is er

17 Dit moet onderscheiden worden van het vraagstuk van de publieke opinie (Bottoms 1995, p. 40). Dat politici en beleidsmakers als uitgangspunt nemen dat 'het publiek' zwaardere straffen wil, wil nog helemaal niet zeggen dat dat ook daadwerkelijk zo is en wordt ook meestal niet empirisch onderbouwd. Zie voor een stand van zaken de oratie van Elffers (2008).

een directe relatie tussen het vertrouwen dat burgers zeggen te hebben in het rechtssysteem en elkaar en de detentieratio. Volgens Lappi-Seppällä is de verklaring voor deze resultaten niet zo ingewikkeld: een gezelschap van 'gelijken' dat zich om het welbevinden van anderen bekommert, zal immers minder bereid zijn, zijn 'medeleden met harde sancties te bestraffen dan een gezelschap waarin grote afstand is tussen de verschillende groepen en waar de bestraffingen vooral "de anderen" betreffen' (Lappi-Seppällä 2010).

Een tweede categorie wordt gevormd door de personen die niet zozeer omdat ze slecht zijn, maar omdat ze terecht of onterecht als gevaarlijk worden beschouwd voor langere tijd buiten de samenleving worden gesloten. Bescherming van de samenleving tegen een gevaarlijke dader was altijd al een grond en legitimatie voor het toepassen van strafrechtelijke sancties, maar wat veranderd is, enerzijds, is dat die gevaarlijkheid veel meer op grond van groepskenmerken wordt vastgesteld dan op basis van individuele kenmerken, en anderzijds dat er een verschuiving heeft plaatsgevonden in het evenwicht tussen *false positives* en *false negatives* (Hudson 2002; Feeley & Simon 1994). Dat wil zeggen: we laten liever iemand langer vastzitten die in de toekomst niet zou hebben gerecidiveerd, hoewel we dat nooit met zekerheid zullen kunnen vaststellen natuurlijk, dan dat we het risico nemen dat we iemand vrijlaten die toch opnieuw strafbare feiten pleegt. Concreet betekenen deze veranderingen in Nederland, maar ook in de meeste andere Europese landen, dat gevaarlijkheid niet langer wordt vastgesteld op basis van een gesprek of gesprekken met gedragsdeskundigen zoals psychologen en psychiaters, maar aan de hand van een lijst met risicofactoren waarbij in het beste geval wel en in het slechtste geval niet het klinische oordeel van een deskundige betrokken wordt (Simon & Feeley 1992; Van Swaaningen 1996 Moerings 2003). Men komt ook eerder dan vroeger tot de vaststelling dat een risico 'onaanvaardbaar' is, wat bijvoorbeeld blijkt uit de grotere terughoudendheid bij het toekennen van proefverlofaan tbs-gestelden (Dienst Justitiële Inrichtingen 2010, p. 23), en de hierboven al beschreven ontwikkelingen ten aanzien van de long stay. Als gevolg van al deze maatregelen verblijft iemand die in 1999 ingestroomd is in de tbs, nu gemiddeld 10,2 jaar in de tbs, terwijl iemand die in 1990 is ingestroomd, daar gemiddeld 7,3 jaar verbleef. In dit getal is niet de verblijfsduur betrokken van de personen die op het moment van deze berekening nog in de tbs verbleven. Van de populatie die in 2000 is gestart, bleek in 2010 nog geen 50% te zijn uitgestroomd (Dienst Justitiële Inrichtingen 2012, p. 27). Bovendien geeft het getal nog geen uitdrukking aan de meest actuele ontwikkelingen, zodat verwacht wordt dat de gemiddelde verblijfsduur nog zal toenemen als die berekend wordt voor latere instroommomenten. Het zijn deze cijfers die delictplegers huiverig maken om zich te laten onderzoeken op hun toerekeningsvatbaarheid en advocaten motiveren om hen daarbij te ondersteunen (Muis & Van der Geest 2010).

In één adem met de gevaarlijken worden vaak de zondebokken genoemd, de derde categorie. Dat is verklaarbaar: naarmate gevaarlijkheid meer op basis van groepskenmerken wordt vastgesteld en de definitie van gevaarlijkheid ruimer wordt, wordt het onderscheid tussen wie terecht en wie ten onrechte als gevaarlijk wordt beschouwd diffuser. Maar het sentiment achter de ene dan wel de andere vorm van uitsluiting verschilt toch wezenlijk. Als zondebokken benoemde ik hierboven de gedetineerden zonder verblijfsvergunning en drugskoeriers. Ze onderscheiden zich in mijn indeling van de categorie gevaarlijke delictplegers omdat er eigenlijk nauwelijks individuele kenmerken zijn waarop hun andere behandeling wordt gebaseerd. Het onderscheid wordt gelegitimeerd met een beroep op een aantal in het oog springende groepskenmerken, zoals het soort delict dat is gepleegd, het land van herkomst of het wel of niet hebben van een verblijfsstatus. Het is ook minder evident dat angst of het vermijden van risico's de grondslag van het onderscheid is. Aan het zondebokmechanisme wordt vaak een durkheimiaanse functie toegeschreven. Door personen of groepen in de samenleving aan te wijzen die er niet bij horen, wordt het saamhorigheidsgevoel van de overige leden versterkt.

Tot de vierde categorie behoren de delictplegers die worden beschouwd als ongemotiveerd om te veranderen of niet in staat om verantwoordelijkheid te nemen voor hun gedrag, de onwaardigen zou men ze kunnen noemen. Zij worden geacht geen resocialiserende inspanningen te verdienen, omdat ze eerdere kansen verpestten, ze zich niet aan afspraken houden of zich anderszins ongemotiveerd opstellen. Met name in de jongste plannen over de 'modernisering van het gevangeniswezen' wordt dit uitgangspunt ver doorgevoerd. 'Er wordt alleen in gedetineerden geïnvesteerd, zoals door het aanbieden van gedragsinterventies, scholing en terugkeeractiviteiten, als kans op succes aanwezig is en als de motivatie en/of houding van de gedetineerde hiertoe aanleiding geeft.'[18] Het is mijns inziens de meest opvallende categorie. Niet alleen omdat ik nergens zo'n obsessieve aandacht voor dit criterium ben tegengekomen als in Nederland, maar ook omdat het hameren op de eigen verantwoordelijkheid van delictsplegers haaks lijkt te staan op het aanwijzen van neurobiologische en andere schijnbaar onveranderbare factoren als dominante verklaring voor crimineel gedrag, een contradictie waarop ook Schuyt onlangs wees in zijn Koningsberger-lezing (Schuyt 2011) en eerder al Barbara Hudson (2003).

Insluiting

Zoals ik al zei, de theoretische verklaringen voor de verharding in de sanctietoepassing zijn veel beter uitgewerkt dan die voor de toch ook indrukwekkende ontwikkeling

18 Zie de brief van de staatssecretaris van justitie over het project Modernisering Gevangeniswezen. *Kamerstukken II* 2010/2011, 29 270, nr. 52 (Brief van 8 november 2011).

aan de zachte kant van het spectrum. Want is het niet even verwonderlijk dat er steeds weer nieuwe vormen van straffen worden geïntroduceerd die wel verbetering van de delictpleger of zijn omstandigheden beogen met als doel hem een betere positie in de samenleving te geven? Toch zijn de theoretische verklaringen voor dit verschijnsel schaars en, voor zover ze er zijn, niet erg diepgaand uitgewerkt. Een eerste verklaring ligt besloten in het begrip *bifurcation* zelf. *Bifurcation* wordt beschreven als een strategie, een strategie waarbij ter compensatie van het opleggen van steeds strengere straffen aan daders die zeer ernstige delicten hebben gepleegd, minder ingrijpende sancties worden ontwikkeld en toegepast op plegers van minder ernstige delicten (Bottoms 1977, 1995; Cavadino & Dignan 2006). Aan het ontwikkelen van lichtere, insluitende straffen ligt volgens deze redenering dus een economisch motief ten grondslag. Er worden lichte straffen toegepast om geld en cellen vrij te maken voor de meest ernstige delictplegers. Kenmerkend voor *bifurcation* is dat tegelijkertijd met het verzwaren van de straffen voor de ernstige delicten, de straffen voor minder ernstige delictplegers substantieel worden verlaagd.

Een tweede verklaring is dat het bij het ontwikkelen en toepassen van straffen die buiten de gevangenis ten uitvoer kunnen worden gelegd, om een verdere uitbreiding van staatscontrole gaat die niet wezenlijk verschilt van de controle die wordt toegepast door mensen op te sluiten. Foucault benoemde de gevangenis als een instituut dat voortkwam uit de wens de bevolking te disciplineren en toezicht te houden op die bevolkingsgroepen die zich aan de minder ingrijpende vormen van disciplinering van toezicht dreigden te onttrekken (Foucault 1975). Alternatieven voor de gevangenisstraf vormen geen breuk met dat streven. Integendeel, het gaat in wezen om een diepgaandere en uitgebreidere vorm van staatsinterventie, omdat die zich nu ook uitstrekt tot plaatsen die normaal tot het privédomein van de burger behoren, het gezin, de school, het werk (Cohen 1979, 1985; Mathiessen 1986). Stanley Cohen zag de ontwikkeling van alternatieven voor de gevangenisstraf dan ook als de voorbode of als de realisatie van 'the punitive city' die Foucault al had voorspeld. En ook de naamgevers van de nieuwe penologie, Simon en Feeley, zien het ontstaan van straffen die in de samenleving ten uitvoer kunnen worden gelegd, juist als bewijs voor hun stelling dat de praktijk van het straffen niet langer gekenmerkt wordt door de wens individuele wetsovertreders te rehabiliteren, maar door het streven criminaliteit effectief te managen door risicovolle groepen te detecteren en ze vervolgens onder toezicht te stellen (Simon & Feeley 1992, p. 40). Als belangrijkste bewijs voor hun claim dat de latente functies van alternatieven voor de gevangenisstraf dominant zijn aan de manifeste, wijzen zij er bij voortduring op dat het alternatieve karakter ook niet wordt waargemaakt. Steeds weer blijkt uit onderzoek dat als alternatieven gepresenteerde sanctiemodaliteiten een aanzuigende werking of een *net-widening*-effect hebben, waarmee wordt bedoeld dat de alternatieven juist of in ieder geval ten dele worden

toegepast in gevallen waar vroeger geen of een minder zware sanctie zou zijn toegepast (Simon & Feeley 1992, p. 439).

Herman Franke verzuchtte in zijn magistrale epos over de geschiedenis van de gevangenisstraf dat hij niet zoveel op had met macro-sociologische verklaringen voor ontwikkelingen van het gevangeniswezen die de nadruk leggen op de slechte bedoelingen van (leden van) de heersende klasse die uit economische eigenbelang de belangrijkste strafveranderingen willens en wetens doorvoeren (Franke 1990, p. 762). Ze hadden hem te veel een samenzwerings- of complotkarakter. Is dan niemand op de gedachte gekomen, zo vroeg hij zich af met betrekking tot de invoering van het cellulaire systeem, dat gevangenishervormers en politici er daadwerkelijk van overtuigd waren dat dit dé oplossing was voor het criminaliteitsprobleem (Franke 2007, p. 23)? De sterkere (rechts)positie van de gevangenen en de ontwikkeling van mildere vormen van (de tenuitvoerlegging van) de gevangenisstraf waren in zijn ogen een rechtstreeks gevolg van het door Elias blootgelegde civilisatieproces (Elias 1936/1980, 2001). De noodzaak die het complexer worden van de samenleving met zich bracht om zich meer in elkaar te verplaatsen, leidde ook tot een grotere gevoeligheid voor het leed van gevangenen. Diezelfde gevoeligheid maakte het ook moeilijker leedtoevoeging op zichzelf te legitimeren. Naast leedtoevoeging, vergelding en afschrikking werd vanaf de tweede helft van de negentiende eeuw ook verbetering van de dader aangevoerd als belangrijke rechtvaardiging voor het opleggen van straffen (Franke 2007, p. 34-35). Dat past ook in de notie van Van Ruller dat straffen rationeel moesten zijn, dat wil zeggen een effectieve bijdrage moesten leveren aan de bestrijding van criminaliteit (Van Ruller 1993, p. 340 e.v.). De civilisatietheorie kan ook de impuls verklaren die de toepassing van sancties buiten de gevangenis in de jaren zeventig van de vorige eeuw kreeg. Uit de publicatie van buitenlands en schaars Nederlands onderzoek bleek in diezelfde periode dat de resultaten van het resocialisatiestreven *in* de gevangenis behoorlijk tegenvielen (Boone 2007, p. 233-234). Gek genoeg, constateert ook Franke, zette dat de gevangenisstraf alleen maar meer onder druk (Franke 2007, p. 36). Nu ook een andere tenuitvoerlegging van de straf niet bleek bij te dragen aan de verbetering van degenen die hem ondergingen, kwam de gevangenisstraf zelf juist onder druk te staan en ging men naarstig op zoek naar alternatieven die wel tegemoet konden komen aan het verlangen naar effectieve straffen.

Ik sluit me grotendeels aan bij de visie van Franke. De zoektocht naar minder ingrijpende sancties dan de vrijheidsbenemende, komt primair voort uit de historisch verklaarbare wens dat met straffen ook iets positiefs moet worden bereikt. Dat na alle mislukkingen steeds weer opnieuw naar sanctievormen wordt gezocht die vooral tot doel hebben resocialisatie en re-integratie te bevorderen, is in theoretisch opzicht

minstens zo fascinerend als de harde kant van *bifurcation*.[19] Dat bepaalde groepen stelselmatig van deze sanctiemodaliteiten worden uitgesloten, zie ik minder als het resultaat van een bewuste strategie (ergo: de visie-Cohen) dan als 'onbedoelde gevolgen van menselijke strevingen' (ergo: de visie-Franke 1990,p. 761). Wel lijkt het van het grootste belang de mechanismen die dit verschijnsel veroorzaken zorgvuldig te onderzoeken, een gedachte die wordt uitgewerkt in de volgende paragraaf.

Microniveau

Hoezeer de theorievorming rondom de risicosamenleving ook inzicht kan geven in de vorm die de sanctietoepassing in Nederland heeft aangenomen, de inzichten moeten noodzakelijk worden aangevuld met meer precieze empirische vaststellingen op microniveau. Met microniveau bedoel ik het niveau van de individuele beslissers. Waar het gaat om de toepassing van straffen, kunnen hiertoe zowel rechters, officieren van justitie, reclasseringswerkers als personeel van penitentiaire instellingen toe gerekend worden. Of iemand wel of niet een werkstraf of een voorwaardelijke straf krijgt, geselecteerd wordt voor een penitentiair programma of een gedragsinterventie, ligt meestal immers niet vast in algemene regelgeving en beleid, maar is een beslissing van een individuele functionaris die vaak een ruime beslissingsvrijheid heeft. Hoe komen zij tot de beslissing een inclusieve dan wel exclusieve straf toe te passen? Hoe passen zij regels toe en hoe worden zij beïnvloed door de macrosociologische ontwikkelingen, zoals ze hiervoor zijn geschetst? Garland zelf waarschuwde al dat op theorie gebaseerde discussies over het veranderde strafrechtelijke klimaat als een basis en niet als een substituut voor empirische analyses moest worden beschouwd (Garland 1997, p. 204; Robinson 2002, p. 6). Ook de constatering dat de processen van uitsluiting die worden toegeschreven aan de veranderende samenleving, zich niet overal in gelijke mate voordoen (Snacken 2011), dwingt tot meer precieze empirische vaststellingen van de condities waaronder dergelijke processen zich voltrekken. Comparatief onderzoek dat ik met mijn buitenlandse collega's zal verrichten in het kader van onze door de Europese Unie gefinancierde netwerksubsidie,[20] maar ook vergelijkend onderzoek tussen verschillende organisaties binnen één staat, laten zien dat organisaties kunnen verschillen in de mate waarin ze gevoelig zijn voor de druk die uitgaat van een verhardend strafklimaat.[21] Het Nederlandse onderzoek naar besluitvormings-

19 Dat steeds meer sanctievormen worden ontwikkeld die uitsluitend incapacitatie beogen, dat wil zeggen het beperken of onmogelijk maken van het plegen van criminaliteit, zonder dat daarmee een andere doelstelling beoogd wordt, bewijst dat het voortzetten van die zoektocht geen vanzelfsprekendheid is. Malsch en Duker publiceren hier binnenkort een bundel over (Malsch & Duker).

20 COST Action IS 1106, Offender Supervision in Europe.

21 Een opvallend resultaat van het onderzoek dat ik met Moerings verrichtte naar de toename van de detentieratio in Nederland, was bijvoorbeeld dat het openbaar ministerie in de periode tussen 1985 en 2005 veel meer invloed heeft gehad op de trend van meer opsluiten dan de politie of de rechter (Boone & Moerings 2007; idem Vollaard & Molenaar 2009).

processen van strafrechtfunctionarissen is schaars, zeker in het licht van de processen van insluiting en uitsluiting, zoals hiervoor geschetst.[22] Uit het rijkere buitenlandse onderzoek destilleer ik behalve het hiervoor geschetste macrosociologisch perspectief, meestal aangeduid als het *penal discourse*,[23] twee andere invloedssferen, die dat besluitvormingsproces beïnvloeden. Het betreft de invloed van de organisatie en organisatiecultuur, het bestuurlijk-organisatorisch perspectief, en de complexe invloed die regels en de beginselen en uitgangspunten die eraan ten grondslag liggen, hebben op de besluitvorming en de uitkomst daarvan, het juridisch perspectief. Ik geef drie voorbeelden van eigen onderzoek, waarin die verschillende invloedssferen goed naar voren komen.

De klassieke studie op het gebied van besluitvorming door uitvoerende functionarissen is *Street-Level Bureaucracy* van Michael Lipsky (1980). Hierin beschrijft hij het spanningsveld tussen managers en uitvoerend werkers in dienstverlenende organisaties zoals de sociale dienst en de politie. Waar managers prioriteit geven aan de grote aantallen, hechten uitvoerend werkers meer belang aan het bieden van kwaliteit aan hun cliënt. Om aan dit voortdurende dilemma het hoofd te kunnen bieden zoeken uitvoerend werkers vaak hun toevlucht tot aanpassingsstrategieën, waaronder afroming of selectie van cliënten. Zij geven daarbij meestal de voorkeur aan cliënten bij wie de kans groot is dat ze er – in termen van de organisatie – succes mee kunnen behalen. In mijn onderzoek uit 2002 naar de toegankelijkheid en kwaliteit van het reclasseringswerk voor cliënten, afkomstig uit etnische minderheidsgroepen, kwam ik vele voorbeelden tegen van afromen (Boone 2002). Dat ging vaak ten koste van cliënten

22 Waar het gaat om het verwante, maar qua reikwijdte beperktere onderzoek naar selectiviteit op basis van sociale klasse, inclusief etnische achtergrond, heeft Rovers in 1999 een overzichtsstudie gepubliceerd. Hij constateert dat het meeste onderzoek gedateerd is, gebaseerd is op kwantitatieve bronnen en de uitkomst van besluitvorming als onderwerp heeft (of er sprake is van selectiviteit) in plaats van het besluitvormingsproces zelf (Rovers 1999).

23 Met name Engelse en Schotse onderzoekers hebben een mooie reeks studies verricht naar de invloed van het penal discourse, concreet het denken in termen van risico en veiligheid op de besluitvorming van reclasseringswerkers. Om dat te onderzoeken maakten ze onder andere gebruik van 'shadow writing', een onderzoekstechniek waarbij de onderzoeker ook een voorlichtingsrapport opstelt om vervolgens diepgaand met de reclasseringswerker in discussie te kunnen gaan over de inhoud en verschillen tussen beide rapporten (Halliday et al. 2008). Hun algemene conclusie is dat risico zelfs in kwantitatief opzicht maar een marginale rol speelt bij de opstelling van voorlichtingsrapporten aan de rechter. Voor zover risico-assessment aan de basis lag van een advies, kon een hoog risico op recidive niet alleen als argument gebruikt worden om af te zien van een reclasseringsinterventie, maar ook als een pleidooi ervoor. In het eerste geval werd de redenering gevolgd dat een straf die ten uitvoer werd gelegd in de samenleving, een te groot veiligheidsrisico opleverde, in het tweede geval dat een reclasseringsinterventie een noodzakelijke voorwaarde was om het recidiverisico te verminderen. De onderzoekers concluderen dat reclasseringswerkers nog steeds proberen tot een professioneel oordeel te komen over de veranderbaarheid of oncorrigeerbaarheid van de delictpleger. Hoewel de terminologie met behulp waarvan deze vaststelling moet plaatsvinden gemoderniseerd is, betreft het nog steeds de aloude taak van het selecteren voor of uitsluiten van delictplegers van mildheid (McNeill et al. 2009, p. 429). Die selectie wordt echter niet louter of overwegend op basis van actuariële overwegingen gemaakt (Robinson 2002, p. 16-17). Tot die conclusie komt ook Marjolein Huizinga in haar scriptie naar de wijze waarop reclasseringswerkers tot een indicatiestelling komen en de rol van het responsiviteitsbeginsel daarin (Huizinga 2011).

afkomstig uit etnische minderheidsgroepen, niet vanwege hun andere etnische achtergrond, maar omdat zij vaker dan andere cliënten eigenschappen bezaten die hen voor de reclassering tot een moeilijke doelgroep maakten. Ze spraken de taal niet of minder goed, ontkenden het delict vaker en waren minder makkelijk te motiveren zich aan te passen aan de Nederlandse samenleving. De hoge productiedruk die er op dat moment binnen de reclassering was, had tot gevolg dat die eigenschappen aan een volwaardig reclasseringsaanbod in de weg stonden. Verdachten werden niet bezocht in de vroeghulp op het politiebureau, omdat ze de taal niet spraken of het delict ontkenden. Er werden substantieel minder voorlichtingsrapporten geschreven en als er wel een rapport werd geschreven, werd vaker verzuimd met een referent uit de naaste omgeving te spreken.[24] Lipsky's meesterwerk is door velen bejubeld, maar er zijn ook veel correcties en aanvullingen op aangebracht.[25] Alleen al vanwege de omvorming van verschillende organisaties binnen de strafrechtspleging naar output gestuurde organisaties moet het voor het bestuderen van besluitvorming binnen die organisaties mijns inziens onverminderd van betekenis worden geacht.

Regels en richtlijnen die proberen vrije beslisruimte van strafrechtelijke functionarissen in te perken, worden vaak verdedigd met een beroep op de noodzaak tot het vergroten van de formele rechtsgelijkheid. Rechtssociologisch onderzoek laat zien dat een te grote nadruk op formele rechtsgelijkheid de materiële rechtsongelijkheid ook juist kan vergroten en sociale ongelijkheid kan versterken (Boone 2004; Boone & Korf 2010). Straftoemetingsrichtlijnen kunnen die consequentie hebben. Alleen over wat meetbaar en kwantificeerbaar is, kunnen immers afspraken worden gemaakt, en wanneer eenheid is gebaseerd op verkeerde gronden, draagt dit evenzeer bij aan rechtsongelijkheid dan wanneer ongegronde verschillen worden geconstateerd (Loth 2001, p. 111). Het hanteren van het gewicht van de vervoerde drugs als uitgangspunt bij de berechting van drugssmokkelaars lijkt een schoolvoorbeeld van dat gevaar. In mijn onderzoek uit 2004 naar de toepassing van straftoemetingsrichtlijnen bij de berechting van cocaïnesmokkelaars kwam naar voren dat de voorzitters van de rechtbanken die betrokken waren bij de berechting van op Schiphol betrapte drugskoeriers, ook zelf vonden dat de door hen opgestelde straftoemetingsrichtlijnen tot té rigide uitkomsten leiden (Boone 2004). Voorstellen om de richtlijnen te versoepelen en meer ruimte in te bouwen voor het meewegen van individuele factoren werden echter niet door alle rech-

24 Een van de meest interessante uitkomsten van het onderzoek was overigens dat er ook reclasseringswerkers waren die zich absoluut niet tot afroming lieten verleiden. Zij spanden zich tot het uiterste in om ook de moeilijk toegankelijke groep cliënten te bereiken en een reclasseringsaanbod te doen zonder dat dat ten koste ging van de te behalen productie. Voor die extra inspanningen werden zij door de organisatie waarvoor zij werkten, echter niet beloond, precies zoals Lipsky voorspelt.

25 Evans vindt bijvoorbeeld dat Lipsky een te eendimensionale kijk heeft op de relatie tussen managers en uitvoerend werkers en wijst in zijn analyse op de vergeten rol van professionaliteit (Evans 2011). Halliday et al. wijzen op het belang van interprofessioneel werken ('de ketenbenadering') voor de theorievorming rondom 'street level bureaucracies' (Halliday et al. 2009).

ters met gejuich ontvangen. De productiedruk was op dat moment immers hoog als gevolg van het bombardement aan cocaïnesmokkelaars dat de georganiseerde misdaad op de luchthaven afvuurde, en strakke richtlijnen hielpen hen juist die stroom aan zaken efficiënt af te doen. Kwantitatieve toetsing van de op dit onderzoek gebaseerde hypothesen (samen met Dirk Korf) liet zien dat de rechters nog wel degelijk in een substantieel aantal gevallen afweken van de richtlijnen. Die toetsing bevestigde echter ook dat richtlijnen kunnen bijdragen aan het vergroten van sociale rechtsongelijkheid. Voor in Nederland geboren verdachten werd twee keer zo vaak naar beneden afgeweken van de richtlijn dan voor in het buitenland geboren verdachten (Boone & Korf 2010).

In het strafrecht en sanctierecht zelf zijn weerstanden ingebouwd tegen een té veelvuldige of anderszins disproportionele toepassing ervan. Ik wijs bijvoorbeeld op het schuldbeginsel, het ultimum remedium-beginsel en het beginsel van minimale beperkingen die er alle in de kern op neerkomen dat het strafrecht en vooral de gevangenisstraf met mate moeten worden toegepast, zoals zo adequaat uitgedrukt door mijn promotor Kelk en zijn mede-auteur Jörg (Jörg, Kelk, Klip 2012). Besluitvorming van strafrechtfunctionarissen vindt plaats in het spanningsveld tussen die in het strafrecht ingebouwde weerstanden en de opwaartse druk die op het strafrecht wordt uitgeoefend door ontwikkelingen in het strafklimaat, zoals hiervoor geschetst en efficiency-eisen die door de organisatie worden gesteld. Dat laatste werd bijvoorbeeld zichtbaar in een onderzoek dat ik in met mijn Utrechtse collega's deed naar de mate waarin de rechter gebruikmaakt van de wettelijke bevoegdheden die hij heeft om invloed uit te oefenen op de tenuitvoerlegging van sancties. We observeerden zittingen en vroegen de rechter vervolgens naar de achtergrond van de beslissingen die hij of zij had genomen. Een van de bevindingen was dat rechters belangrijke bevoegdheden die hij had, structureel niet benutte met als argument dat hij de overige procesdeelnemers, knarsetandend 'ketenpartners' genoemd, niet voor de voeten wilde lopen. Hoewel hij er in sommige zaken van overtuigd was dat een voorwaardelijke straf met reclasseringstoezicht beter op zijn plaats was dan een onvoorwaardelijke straf, liet hij dat achterwege als er geen reclasseringsvoorstel lag van die strekking. De reclassering wilde immers niet met 'cadeaugevallen' worden opgescheept, dat wil zeggen zaken waarover zij zelf niet positief hadden geadviseerd. Ook schikte de rechter zich in de beleidsafspraken die tussen het openbaar ministerie en de reclassering waren gemaakt over het soort zaken waarin advies over een verdachte werd ingewonnen, met als consequentie dat de rechter de exclusiefactoren die door de reclassering en het openbaar ministerie werden gehanteerd, automatisch overnam (Boone et al. 2009).

Wie resocialisatie, gedragsverandering of desnoods alleen recidivevermindering beschouwt als een belangrijke doelstelling van de sanctietoepassing, en het huidige beleid duidt daar mijns inziens op, zou zich de categorische uitsluiting van de groepen

delictplegers, zoals hierboven benoemd, moeten aantrekken. De vraag hoe strafrechtfunctionarissen tot hun beslissing komen en onder welke omstandigheden dit leidt tot (het afbreken van) een insluitende dan wel uitsluitende sanctie dient daarom onderwerp te zijn van systematisch onderzoek. Grootschalig, kwantitatief onderzoek naar de uitkomst van beslissingsprocessen zal niet veel meer opleveren dan een reproductie van de gegevens die we inmiddels kennen. Kwalitatief en etnografisch onderzoek naar de wijze waarop besluitvorming plaatsvindt kan duidelijk maken welke belemmeringen aan het opleggen dan wel laten voortduren van insluitende sancties aan de genoemde categorieën delictplegers in de weg staat en naar de omstandigheden, waaronder die belemmeringen in individuele gevallen kunnen worden overwonnen.

Normatief oordeel

Dan kom ik nu aan de laatste twee vragen die ik in deze oratie wil beantwoorden: moet *bifurcation* wel als een onwenselijk verschijnsel worden beschouwd, en zo ja, kunnen we er iets aan doen? Om met de eerste vraag te beginnen. Op het eerste oog heeft het wel een zekere logica dat de zwaarste straffen worden gereserveerd voor de grootste of gevaarlijkste delictplegers, terwijl mildere en meer insluitende sanctievormen worden toegepast op minder gevaarlijke en ernstige delictplegers. Dit erkent ook de aangever van het begrip, Bottoms,[26] en in Nederland beschouwt Van Stokkom beleid dat zware straffen reserveert voor ernstige en gewoontemisdadigers en lichte voor gelegenheidscriminelen, in principe als een vorm van pragmatisch sanctiebeleid (Van Stokkom 1999, p. 42). In het voorgaande heb ik nu juist proberen aan te tonen dat de lijn tussen harde en zachte straffen bepaald niet parallel loopt met die tussen ernstige en minder ernstige delictplegers en zelfs niet met die tussen gevaarlijke en minder gevaarlijke delinquenten, zoals de theorievorming rond de risicosamenleving lijkt te suggereren. De verklaring voor de toepassing van uitsluitende dan wel insluitende sanctievormen moet veel meer gevonden worden in de kracht van wereldwijde maatschappelijke uitsluitingsprocessen van bepaalde groepen en het mechanisme kansrijke delictplegers voorrang te geven boven kansarme. Tegen deze praktijk zijn zowel praktische als principieel-juridische argumenten aan te voeren.

Voor wat betreft het praktische bezwaar: Ik heb in deze rede niet alleen de verharding van het strafklimaat willen benadrukken, maar juist ook willen laten zien dat er gelijktijdig steeds weer nieuwe initiatieven genomen worden om strafrechtelijke interventies te ontwikkelen die een positieve uitwerking hebben op gedrag en de positie van de delictpleger in de samenleving verbeteren. Desondanks is het nogal onlogisch

26 Maar, stelt Bottoms al in 1977: 'if this bifurcation is to be the keystone of future policy, it only raises the more starkly the problem as to what and who are to be deemed to be "grave crimes" and "serious offenders". And there is at present no hint of any adequate theoretical justification in this area' (Bottoms 1977, p. 91).

en contraproductief wanneer onderzoek keer op keer aantoont dat sancties die primair worden ingezet om de recidive te verminderen, overwegend worden toegepast op delictplegers die ze het minste nodig hebben. Even contraproductief, om niet te zeggen immoreel, is het voor strafbare feiten veroordeelde vreemdelingen geen Nederlands te leren of andere activiteiten aan te bieden die hen voorbereiden op de terugkeer naar welk land ook, onder het mom dat ze na hun detentie het land moeten verlaten, terwijl onderzoek keer op keer aantoont dat een substantieel deel uiteindelijk in Nederland blijft en de Hoge Raad deze redenering al in 1987 naar de prullenbak heeft verwezen (Boone & Kox 2012).

Tegen sommige uitwassen van de sanctietoepassing, zoals hierboven beschreven, zijn tal van juridische bezwaren aan te voeren en ook aangevoerd. 'To do justice to the ultra-other, we need to put rights at the centre of our models of justice', zegt Hudson terecht (Hudson 2003, p. 213), en ook Snacken doet de oproep *human rights*-instrumenten in te zetten om tot een meer reductionistische strafrechtelijke politiek te komen (Snacken 2010, p. 275). Een overkoepelend argument tegen de vorm die *bifurcation* in Nederland heeft aangenomen, vind ik in het recht op resocialisatie. Hoeveel omstreden is zo'n recht rechtstreeks af te leiden uit artikel 10 lid 3 van het Internationaal Verdrag Inzake Burgerlijke en Politieke Rechten, een artikel waarop Nederland geen voorbehoud heeft gemaakt.[27] In Nederland wordt resocialisatie primair benaderd als een doel van straffen. Die benadering maakt de constatering dat het moet worden afgeschaft of bijgesteld voor bepaalde groepen als het onvoldoende wordt bereikt, al snel tot een legitieme redenering. Ik heb echter niet zo op insluitende sanctievormen gehamerd, omdat ik per se geloof dat die een substantiële bijdrage leveren aan het terugdringen van recidive, de enge betekenis die meestal aan het resocialisatiestreven wordt gegeven. De succespercentages die worden behaald, zijn meestal bescheiden,[28] en dat verbaast niet als men daarbij in ogenschouw neemt in welke miserabele toestand veel personen zich bevinden die met het strafrecht in aanraking komen, zoals hiervoor geschetst. Los van het te behalen effect pleit ik voor de erkenning van een recht op resocialisatie, zoals dat al door het Duitse Federale Constitutionele Hof in 1973 is gedaan. Het hof baseerde die erkenning op het grondwettelijk erkende recht van menselijke waardigheid en vrijheid van ontplooiing en op de verplichting van de staat om die personen in de samenleving bij te staan die 'vanwege hun persoonlijke zwakheid, schuld, onvermogen of sociale achterstelling werden beperkt in hun maatschappelijke ontwikkeling'. Tot die groep rekende het hof ook gedetineerden en ex-gedetineerden (Morgenstern 2011, p. 21-22). Erkenning van een dergelijk recht lost de problemen die zich voordoen bij de realisatie ervan natuurlijk niet op, maar maakt wel dat personen niet zomaar van resocialiserende inspanningen

27 Met dank aan Gerard de Jonge.

28 Hermanns (2009) noemt een reductie van recidive van 8,2% voor de meest succesvolle interventies.

kunnen worden uitgesloten met het argument dat ze niet tot een bepaalde doelgroep behoren of geacht worden hun kansen te hebben verspeeld.

Afsluiting

Kunnen we er iets aan doen, was de laatste vraag die ik in de inleiding stelde. Ik ben een universitair onderzoeker en de universiteiten bevinden zich in financieel moeilijk vaarwater, dus mijn antwoord ligt voor de hand: meer onderzoek. Samen met mijn studenten, junior-onderzoekers, toekomstige promovendi, binnenlandse en buitenlandse collega's hoop ik in de komende jaren meer onderzoek te doen naar de processen van insluiting en uitsluiting, langs de lijnen zoals uiteengezet. Ook door onderzoek te doen naar de verschijnselen die in tegenspraak zijn met de tendensen die ik hiervoor heb geschetst, want daar ben ik het afgelopen halfuur niet aan toegekomen.

Dankwoord

Het protocol van de Rijksuniversiteit Groningen schrijft voor dat aan het eind van een oratie niet bedankt mag worden, zoals dat wel gebruikelijk is aan alle andere universiteiten. Ik heb gevraagd waarom dat zo is. Het bleek dat in het verleden benoemde hoogleraren ellenlange dankwoorden uitspraken en dat wilde men voor de toekomst voorkomen. Dat doel onderschrijf ik, ik zal daarom kort bedanken. Het bestuur van de Rijksuniversiteit Groningen bedank ik voor het in mij gestelde vertrouwen. Berend Keulen voor zijn uitnodiging in Groningen te solliciteren. Esther Gerringa en Martina Althoff voor de geestelijke en fysieke ondersteuning bij het voorbereiden van deze dag. Dina Siegel en Francois Kristen voor de warme en ongecompliceerde wijze waarop jullie mijn benoeming hebben verwelkomd en mogelijk gemaakt. Constantijn Kelk, opnieuw ben je aanwezig op een belangrijke dag in mijn loopbaan, ondanks een haperende gezondheid. Ik ben er trots op jouw promovendus te zijn. Martin Moerings ben ik in zekere zin altijd als mijn dagelijks begeleider blijven beschouwen. Eerder dan ikzelf zagen jullie in dat dit de beste leerstoel voor mij was. Kristel Beyens en Jolande uit Beijerse bedank ik voor het kritisch lezen en becommentariëren van een eerdere versie van deze rede. Lieve Boes. Ondanks jou, schreef ik in het voorwoord van mijn proefschrift en dat vond niet iedereen leuk. Dat jij er hartelijk om kon lachen, gaf me het vertrouwen dat onze toen prille relatie nog wel even voort zou duren, maar de woorden van toen zou ik nu niet meer in mijn mond durven nemen. Lieve Belle en Parel. Jullie zijn natuurlijk de boeven die voor mij op de eerste plaats komen.

Ik heb gezegd.

Literatuur

Bauman, Z. (2000), *Liquid Modernity*, Cambridge: Polity Press.

Beck, U. (1992), *The risk society; toward a new modernity*, London: Sage.

Boone, M. & G. de Jonge (red.) (2001), *De Penitentiaire Beginselenwet in werking. Het gevangeniswezen anno 2001*, Deventer: Gouda Quint.

Boone, M. (2002), *Leren diversifiëren. Reclassering en culturele diversiteit*, Utrecht: Willem Pompe Instituut.

Boone, M. (2003), Penitentiaire Beginselen en de bewaring van vreemdelingen, *PROCES*, (82) 6, p. 301-312.

Boone, M. (2004), Richtlijn of regel? De rechterlijke macht en de bolletjesslikkers, in: M. Boone, R.S.B. Kool, C.M. Pelser & T. Boekhout van Solinge (red.), *Discretie in het strafrecht*, Den Haag: Boom Juridische uitgevers, p. 227-248.

Boone, M. (2006), De Noodwet drugskoeriers als proeftuin voor een grootschalige versobering van het gevangeniswezen, *PROCES*, (85) 4, p. 140-153.

Boone, M. (2007), Selective Rehabilitation, in: M. Boone & M. Moerings (eds.), *Dutch Prisons*, Den Haag: Boom Juridische uitgevers, p. 231-249.

Boone, M. & M. Moerings (2007), Growing Prison Rates, in: M. Boone & M. Moerings (eds.), *Dutch Prisons*, Den Haag: Boom Juridische uitgevers, p. 51-76.

Boone, M. (2009), Er zitten hier alleen moslims. Een bijzondere afdeling voor 'terroristen': Mag het? Werkt het?, in: C. Brants & S. van der Poel, *Diverse kwesties. Liber amicorum prof. dr. Frank Bovenkerk*, Den Haag: Boom Juridische uitgevers, Pompe reeks nr. 56.

Boone, M. (2010), Only for minor offences, Community service in the Netherlands, *European Journal of Probation*, 2 (1), p. 22-40.

Boone, M., A. Beijer, A.A. Franken & C. Kelk (2009), *De tenuitvoerlegging van sancties: maatwerk door de rechter?*, Den Haag: Boom Juridische uitgevers, Pompe reeks nr. 53.

Boone, M. & D.J. Korf (2010), Bestraffing van cocaïnesmokkelaars. Richtlijnen, rechters, rechtbanken en de persoon van de dader, *Tijdschrift voor Criminologie*, (52) 3, p. 239-258.

Boone, M. & M. Kox (2012), What works for irregular migrants in the Netherlands, *European Journal of Probation*, (4) 3, p. 54-68.

Bottoms, A. (1995), The philosophy and politics of punishment and sentencing, in: C. Clarkson & R. Morgan (eds.), *The politics of sentencing reform*, Oxford: Clarendon Press, p. 17-19.

Bottoms, A.E. (1977), Reflections on the renaissance of dangerousness, *Howard Journal of Penology and Crime Prevention*, 16, p. 70-96.

Boutellier, H. (2002), *De veiligheidsutopie*, Den Haag: Boom Juridische uitgevers.

Cavadino, M. & J. Dignan (2006), *Penal systems. A comparative approach*, London: Sage.
Cohen, S. (1979), The punitive city: notes on the dispersal of social control, *Contemporary Crises*, 3 (4), p. 341-363.
Cohen, S. (1985), *Visions of social control: crime, punishment and classification.* Cambridge: Polity Press.
Dienst Justitiële Inrichtingen (2010), *Tbs in getal*, 2005-2009
Dienst Justitiële Inrichtingen (2011a), *Gevangeniswezen in getal 2005-2010.*
Dienst Justitiële Inrichtingen (2011b), *Tbs in getal 2005-2010.*
Dienst Justitiële Inrichtingen (2011c), *Vreemdelingenbewaring in getal, 2007-2011.*
Dienst Justitiële Inrichtingen (2012), *Forensische zorg in getal, 2007-2011.*
Downes, D. & R. van Swaaningen (2007), The Road to Dystopia? Changes in the Penal Climate of the Netherlands, in: M. Tonry & C. Bijleveld (eds.), *Crime and Justice in the Netherlands. Volume 35*, Chicago: The University of Chicago Press, p. 31-71
Elffers, H. (2008), *Een straffe aanpak*, Den Haag: Boom Juridische uitgevers.
Elias, N. (1936/1980), *Über den Prozeß der Zivilisation soziogenetische und psychogenetische Untersuchungen. Erster Band: Wandlungen des Verhaltens in den weltlichen Obersichten des Abendlandes*, Frankfurt am Main: Suhrkamp.
Elias, N. (2001), *Het civilisatieproces. Sociogenetische en psychogenetische onderzoekingen*, Amsterdam: Uitgeverij Boom.
Evans, T. (2011), Professionals, managers and discretion: Critiquing street level bureaucracy, *British Journal of Social Work*, 41, p. 368-386.
Feeley, M. & J. Simon (1994), Actuarial justice: The emerging new criminal law, in: D. Nelken (ed.), *The futures of criminology*, London: Sage, p. 173-201.
Fischer, T., M. Captein & B. Zwirs (2012), *Gedragsinterventies voor volwassen justitiabelen. Stand van zaken en mogelijkheden voor innovatie*, Den Haag: Boom Juridische uitgevers, WODC Onderzoek en Beleid nr. 302.
Fiselier, J. (1998), Lang leve de reclassering, *Sancties*, 4, p. 205-209.
Forum Levenslang (Juni 2010), *Factsheet. Feitelijke gegevens over de levenslange gevangenisstraf.*
Forum Levenlang (Juli 2011), *Update Factsheet. Feitelijke gegevens over de levenslange gevangenisstraf.*
Foucault, M. (1975), *Surveiller et punir. Naissance de la prison*, Paris: Gallimard.
Franke, H. (1990), *Twee eeuwen gevangen: misdaad en straf in Nederland*, Utrecht: Het Spectrum.
Franke, H. (2007), Two centuries of imprisonment: socio-historical explanations, in: M. Boone & M. Moerings (eds.), *Dutch prisons*, The Hague: BJu Legal Publishers, p. 5-51.
Garland, D. (1997), Governmentality and the problem of crime: Foucault, criminology, sociology, *Theoretical Criminology*, 1 (2), p. 173-214.

Garland, D. (2001), *The culture of control. Crime and social order in contemporary society*, Chicago: University of Chicago Press.

Giddens, A. (1990), *The consequences of modernity*, Cambridge: Polity Press.

Halliday, S., N. Burns, N. Hutton, F. McNeill & C. Tata (2008), Shadow writing and participant observation: A study of criminal justice social work around sentencing, *Journal of Law and Society*, 35 (2), 189-213 .

Halliday, S., N. Burns, N. Hutton, F. McNeill & C. Tata (2009), Street-level bureaucracy, interprofessional relations and coping mechanisms: A study of criminal justice social workers in the sentencing process, *Law & Policy*, 32 (4), p. 405-427.

Hermanns, J. (2009), Nieuwe wegen in het terugdringen van recidive?, *PROCES*, (88) 3, 147-154.

Hudson, B. (2002), Punishment and Control, in: M. Maguire, R. Morgan & R. Reiner (red.), *The Oxford handbook of criminology* (third edition), Oxford: Oxford University Press, p. 231-254.

Hudson, B. (2003), *Justice in the risk society: Challenging and re-affirming justice in late modernity*, London: Sage.

Huizinga, M. (2011), *Totstandkoming van een adviesrapportage door reclasseringswerkers*, scriptie master Criminologie, Universiteit Utrecht.

Inspectie voor de sanctietoepassing (2006), *Praktijk penitentiaire programma's*, Inspectierapport Themaonderzoek.

Inspectie voor de sanctietoepassing (2008), *Praktijk penitentiaire programma's*, Inspectiebericht, Vervolgonderzoek.

N. Jörg, Kelk, C. & A.H. Klip (2012), Strafrecht met mate, Deventer, Kluwer (12e druk).

Kalidien, S. & N. de Heer-de Lange (eds.) (2011), *Criminaliteit en rechtshandhaving 2010. Ontwikkelingen en samenhangen*, Den Haag: Boom Juridische uitgevers.

Kalmthout, A.M. van (2007), Het regiem van de vreemdelingenbewaring; de balans na 25 jaar, *Justitiële verkenningen,* 33 (4), p. 89-102.

Kelk, C. (1998), De reclassering van gedetineerden, *Delikt en Delinkwent,* 28 (5), p. 421-426.

Lappi-Sepällä, J. (2010), Finnland, in: F. Dünkel et al. (eds.), *Kriminalität, Kriminalpolitik, strafrechtliche Sanktionspraxis und Gefangenraten im europäischen Vergleich*, Mönchengladbach: Forum Verlag Godesberg, p. 299-366.

Lipsky, M. (1980), *Street-level bureaucracy: Dilemma's of the individual in public services*, New York: Russell Sage Foundation.

Loth, M.A. (2001), Rechterlijke samenwerking en rechtsvinding, in: C.P.M. Cleiren & G.K. Schoep (red.), *Rechterlijke samenwerking*, Deventer: Gouda Quint, E.M. Meijers Instituut, p. 111-120.

Lünneman, K., G. Bijers & M. Wentink (2005), *Werkstraffen: succes verzekerd? Succes- en faalfactoren bij werkstraffen van meerderjarigen.* Utrecht: Verweij-Jonker Instituut.

Malsch, M. & M. Duker (eds.), *Incapacitation Trends and New Perspectives.* Ashgate Publishing LTD.

Mathiessen, T. (1986), The politics of abolition, *Contemporary Crises*, 10 (1), p. 81-94.

McNeill, F., N. Burns, S. Halliday, N. Hutton & C. Tata (2009), Risk, responsibility and reconfiguration: Penal adaptation and misadaptation, *Punishment and Society*, 11 (4), p. 419-442.

Moerings, M., *Straffen met het oog op veiligheid, een onderneming vol risico's*, Oratie Universiteit Leiden 2003.

Morgenstern, C. (2011), Judicial rehabilitation in Germany: The use of criminal records and the removal of recorded convictions, *European Journal of Probation*, 3 (1), p. 20-35.

Muis, K.P.M.A. & L. van der Geest (2010), *TBS uit de gratie*, Utrecht: Nyfer.

Nelissen, P.Ph. (2001), Kansarme en kansrijke gedetineerden, selectiviteit en tweedeling in penitentiaire inrichtingen, *Justitiële verkenningen*, 27 (6), p. 66-76.

Poort, R. (2009), *Fundamenten voor toezicht. Over de grondslagen voor de ontwikkeling van reclasseringstoezicht*, Utrecht: Reclassering Nederland, Stichting Verslavingsreclassering ggz, Leger des Heils.

Pratt, J. (2005), Elias, punishment, and decivilization, in: J. Pratt et al. (eds.), *The new punitiveness, trends, theories, perspectives*, Cullompton: Willan Publishing.

Raad voor Strafrechtstoepassing en Jeugdbescherming (2007), *Advies: De zorg aan gedetineerden met een ernstige psychische stoornis of verslaving.*

Raad voor Strafrechtstoepassing en Jeugdbescherming (2008a), *Advies: Gedetineerden met een verstandelijke beperking.*

Raad voor Strafrechtstoepassing en Jeugdbescherming (2008b), *Advies: Long Stay.*

Raad voor Strafrechtstoepassing en Jeugdbescherming (2010), *Advies: Regimesontwikkeling in inrichtingen voor strafrechtelijk veroordeelde vreemdelingen.*

Raad voor Strafrechtstoepassing en Jeugdbescherming (2011), *Advies: Minimumstraffen voor recidive bij zware minimumstraffen.*

Reidnied, J. (2001), De doelgroep en doelstelling van het penitentiair programma, in: M. Boone & G. de Jonge (red.), *De Penitentiaire Beginselenwet in werking*, Deventer: Gouda Quint, Pompe reeks 35, p. 35-59.

Robinson, G. (2002), Exploring risk management in probation practice: Contemporary developments in England and Wales, *Punishment and Society,* 4 (5), p. 5-24.

Rovers, B. (1999), *Klassenjustitie; overzicht van onderzoek naar selectiviteit in de strafrechtsketen*, Rotterdam: Erasmus Universiteit.

Ruller, S. van (1993), Het irrationele van strafrechtelijke sancties, *Tijdschrift voor Criminologie* 35 (4), p. 336-350.

Sackers, H.J.B. (2011), De afschaffing van de Terroristenafdeling, *Sancties*, 6, p. 333-337.

Schuyt, C.J.M. (2011), *Universitair verzet (1940-1945), maatschappelijk verzet en de waarde van de wetenschap: een drieluik*, Koningsberger-lezing, Universiteit Utrecht, Den Haag: Boom Lemma.

Simon, J. & M.M. Feeley (1992), The new penology: Notes on the emerging strategy of corrections and its implications, *Criminology*, 30 (4), p. 449-474.

Snacken, S. (2010), Resisting punitiveness in Europe, *Theoretical Criminology*, 14 (273), p. 273-291.

Snacken, S. (2011), Conclusion: why and how to resist punitiveness in Europe, in: S. Snacken & E. Dumortier (eds.), *Resisting punitiveness in Europe? Welfare, human rights and democracy*. New York: Routledge, p. 247-260.

Stokkom, B.A.M. van (1999), Pragmatisch sanctiebeleid. Zacht waar het kan, hard waar het moet, *Justitiële verkenningen*, 25 (6), p. 41-56.

Swaaningen, R. van (1996), Justitie als verzekeringsmaatschappij, *Justitiële Verkenningen*, 22 (5), pp. 82-97.

Tonry, M. (eds.) Crime, Punishment and Politics in Comparative Perspective, *Crime and Justice. A Review of Research*, vol. 36, Chicago: University Press.

Tulder, F. van (2011), De straffende rechter, *Nederlands Juristenblad*, 24, p. 1544-1550.

Tulkens, H.J.J. (1988), *Graden van vrijheid*, Arnhem: Gouda Quint.

Veldhuis, T.M. et al. (2010), *Terroristen in detentie. Evaluatie van de terroristenafdeling*, Rijksuniversiteit Groningen, Faculteit Gedrags- en Maatschappijwetenschappen.

Verhagen, J. (2011), *Gedetineerden ontmaskerd. Hoe in Nederland over gedetineerden wordt gedacht en hoe het werkelijk 'zit'*, Veenhuizen: Nationaal Gevangenismuseum.

Vollaard, B.A. & D.E.G. Molenaar (2009), Beperkte invloed rechter op gebruik celstraf, *Nederlands Juristenblad*, 84 (19), p. 1208-1215.

Wermink, H., A. Blokland, P. Nieuwbeerta & N. Tollenaar (2009), Recidive na werkstraffen en na gevangenisstraffen. Een gematchte vergelijking, *Tijdschrift voor Criminologie*, 51 (3), p. 211-228.

Wermink, H., J. de Keijser & P. Schuyt (2012), Verschillen in straftoemeting in soortgelijke zaken. Een kwantitatief onderzoek naar de rol van specifieke kenmerken van de dader, *Nederlands Juristenblad*, (86) 11, p. 727-733.

Wingerden, S.G.C. van & P. Nieuwbeerta (2006), Ontwikkelingen in de lengte van gevangenisstraffen voor moord en doodslag: een trend naar langere straffen. *Trema Tijdschrift voor de Rechterlijke Macht*, 29 (8), p. 329-337.

Young, J. (1999), *The exclusive society: Social exclusion, crime, and difference in late modernity*, London: Sage Publications.